1 MONTH OF
FREE
READING

at

www.ForgottenBooks.com

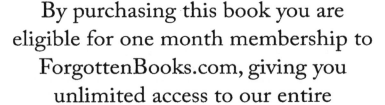

By purchasing this book you are
eligible for one month membership to
ForgottenBooks.com, giving you
unlimited access to our entire
collection of over 1,000,000 titles via
our web site and mobile apps.

To claim your free month visit:
www.forgottenbooks.com/free967038

ISBN 978-0-260-73192-0
PIBN 10967038

Descriptive Trade List,

....of the....

Latest Novelties, Etc.

Convention Hall.

19   03

Nathan Smith & Son

Adrian, Michigan

U. S. A.

TO OUR FRIENDS AND PATRONS.

Again has the privilege been granted us of presenting to you our wholesale catalogue for 1903, and we trust that this will meet with the same welcome, which you have hitherto extended to previous issues. We are still continuing our improvements—this being necessary, owing to our constantly increasing trade—and are in better position to serve you than ever. Our stock is all first-class, which enables us to give to each customer nothing but just treatment. Will do our best to please you.

Chrysanthemums are our specialty, but you will note that we also offer the best varieties of CARNATIONS, CANNAS, GERANIUMS, PELARGONIUMS, &c.

All inquiries will be cheerfully answered to the best of our ability.

Soliciting a share of your patronage in the future, we remain,

Yours very respectfully,

NATHAN SMITH & SON.

READ CAREFULLY BEFORE ORDERING,
THE FOLLOWING TERMS OF SALE:

All previous quotations are canceled by this list.

Not less than **five (5) plants of one variety** at 100 rates, and where dozen rates are given, **six (6) at dozen** and **twenty-five (25) at 100 rates, EXCEPT WHERE OTHERWISE NOTED.**

We do not **bind ourselves** to these prices **after June 1st,** as there is often a decline or advance, according to supply and demand. In case stock of certain varieties is exhausted, we reserve the **right to decline** the order.

While we **exercise** the **greatest care** in executing all orders to keep our stock **true to name,** we give **no warranty, expressed** or **implied, and cannot guarantee** or be in any way **responsible for the crop,** either as to **variety** or **product.** Should errors occur, do not fail to **report at once,** as we **cannot** entertain claims of **long standing.**

All orders are filled in **strict rotation,** carefully labeled, lightly and securely packed, and delivered to the carriers **in good condition** free of charge.

Cash, or satisfactory reference must accompany **all orders** from unknown correspondents. You can **save money** by sending **cash,** as we allow **five (5) per cent. discount** where remittance accompanies the order. If discount is not deducted, we will include extra plants to cover the amount. All accounts are **due and subject to draft in sixty (60) days,** unless otherwise agreed upon.

Those desiring goods shipped **C. O. D.,** are requested to advance a sufficient amount to assure us they will be accepted on delivery. We **ship** all plants by **Express** unless otherwise instructed, but where impracticable, we will forward by Mail post-paid all orders of fifty cents and upwards.

Our shipping facilities are excellent, having direct connections with **all parts of the country. We guarantee** our shipments to be delivered at the **special plant rate,** which is 20 per cent. less than the rate on merchandise.

When ordering, please mention a few additional varieties. These will be sent **only** in cases where the stock of those ordered is exhausted.

To **avoid errors** and delays, make your order on a **separate sheet,** using only **one side,** and **one variety** on a line. To this add your **Name, Post-Office** and **State, plainly written,** also give **Street Number** or **P. O. Box,** if any.

☞ **In all cases the foregoing terms will be strictly adhered to.**

Chrysanthemum Novelties for 1903

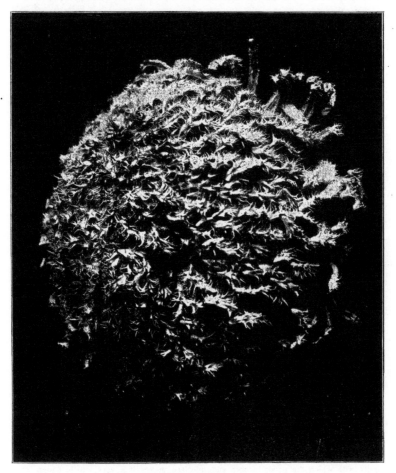

F. J. Taggart.

Before describing our New Chrysanthemums for 1903, we cannot refrain from alluding to our phenomenal success at the exhibitions of the season just closed. Out of 70 entries we were awarded 38 First, 11 Second and 2 Third Premiums, a total of 51; also one Gold and two Bronze Medals. In calling your attention to our novelties for the coming year, will say, they possess the excellent qualities that have characterized our past productions.

We have endeavored, as far as possible, to compare the varieties with others now in commerce, believing this would aid in getting a clearer idea of their character.

Convention Hall.—(The Queen x Merza.) Closely resembles The Queen in stem, foliage and form, but is without the objectionable eye. Color, white, of an exceedingly pure tone. Very broad center petals, incurving closely; tubular ray florets. Height, 4 ft. Second crown bud, maturing Nov. 5. Winner of the $200 prize at Kansas City, 1901. This variety we were unable to disseminate last spring as advertised, owing to limited stock. It is unquestionably the finest white that has been produced for many years, no white excepted. Experts say it is so white that Mrs. Weeks is dirty compared with it, surpassing Timothy Eaton or any other white, in size and contour. Certificate C. S. A., scoring 97 points.

Algoma.—Japanese Incurved, on style of The Queen, producing heavy foliage close under

Algoma.

the flower, with an exceptional short, stiff stem, both from crown and terminal bud. Color, a beautiful shade of light rose, silvery reverse. Best from crown bud, taken after Sept. 1. 4½ ft. high. Certificate C. S. A.

Globosa Alba.—A very compact, closely incurved Japanese, of globular form, and pure white as the name indicates. It is so closely incurved that properly speaking it belongs to the Chinese or Incurved type; 5½ in. in diameter; 4 ft. high. Stem and foliage all that could be desired. Certificate C. S. A.

Sephia.—Large Japanese Incurved. Style of flower and growth similar to Mrs. Park, but has better stem with foliage close to the bloom, and fully double under all conditions. Medium shade of yellow similar to Col. D. Appleton. Best from crown bud after Sept. 1. Stem and foliage excellent. Height, 4 ft. Certificate C. S. A.

Miss Minnie Bailey.—A seedling from Mrs. Perrin, possessing good stem and foliage, but surpassing that variety in fullness, being fully double under all conditions. Color, bright pink, very similar to that of Mrs. Perrin, although a trifle lighter from the influence of Lavender Queen, the other parent. We predict this will become one of the most popular commercial varieties. Height, 3½ ft; size, 5½ in. Certificate C. S. A.

H. W. Buckbee.—(Mrs. T. L. Park x Nagoya.) This variety may be briefly described as an improved Nagoya. It is brighter yellow and in habit more dwarf, with petals more loosely arranged. An excellent commercial variety. Good keeper. Best bud about Sept. 15. Height, 3½ ft. Certificate C. S. A., also S. A. F. Bronze Medal at Chicago.

Mrs. J. J. Mitchell.—A large Japanese Incurved. Color, beautiful, clear cream. The irregularity with which the petals incurve and interlace makes it a very artistic flower. Good stem and foliage; 5 ft.; best from terminal bud. Certificate C. S. A.

Ethelyn.—A Japanese Incurved. Petals, light rose pink at the base, shading lighter at the tips. A very handsome formed flower, which is sure to become popular when well known. Height, 3½ ft.; size, 6 in.; best from terminals taken about Sept. 15.

N. B. This is not the variety certificated at Cincinnati under the name of Ethelyn. That variety showed a tendency to drop its petals, so for the good of the trade and to protect our interests, we thought best to destroy the stock and appropriate the name to one more worthy.

Convention Hall is The Queen of whites.

F. J. Taggart.—The most striking novelty of recent years. The best of all the hairy or plumed section. A great advance over all yellows in this class, being perfectly double and the hair-like filaments more pronounced. No other variety at Kansas City and Chicago attracted so much attention and brought out such exclamations of wonder and surprise. Color, light yellow. Flowers, 8 in. in diameter. An exhibition variety of exceptional merits. Winner of $150 prize and Gold Medal at Kansas City, also Bronze Medal at Chicago.

Ready for distribution March 1st.

Prices are as Follows:

One Plant 60c	Twenty-five Plants . . . . 40c each
Six Plants . . . . 50c each	Fifty Plants . . . . 35c each
Twelve Plants . . . . 45c each	One Hundred Plants . . . . 30c each

Purchasers are at liberty to select as many of each variety as they choose, and the total number ordered will establish the price.

New Chrysanthemums From Various Sources.

Price, 50c each; $5.00 per doz.; $30.00 per 100, except where noted.

Ready for distribution March 1st.

Amorita.—(May.) Mrs. Perrin x Mrs. J. Jones. A bright, clear satin pink, shading to Perrin color at base of petals. An exceedingly attractive incurved flower without being stiff or formal. In season from the 15th of October. Excellent stem, and foliage close up to the flower. Average size, 6 in. in diameter, by 4½ in. deep; height, 3½ to 4 ft. It is of very easy culture, every stem producing a perfect flower. Take either crown or terminal bud. Certificate **C. S. A.** 40c ea.; $4.00 per doz.; $25.00 per 100.

Columbia. — (Hill & Craig.) This variety won first at Chicago for best pink seedling lighter than Morel. It is a variety of exceptional beauty, especially in build, which is perfect. Rounded, incurving blooms similar to Chadwick. Center white, the base a most pleasing shade of pure pink. The petals are of good substance and have a pearl finish. Height, from 4 to 4½ ft.; good foliage and stiff stem. A first-class shipper. Shade after buds begin to expand. Early mid-season and later; take first bud after Sept. 1st.

Estelle. — (H. M. Altick.) A pure white sport from Glory of Pacific, claimed by the originator to be entirely distinct from Polly Rose, being far superior in shape and substance, also ten days earlier than its parent. C. S. A. Certificate. 25c ea.; $2.50 per doz.

Henry Sinclair.—(May.) H. L. Sunderbruch x Jeannie Falconer. Color, clear bright canary yellow. Handsome globular flower, 6 in. in diameter by 5 in. deep. In season Oct. 15th, and can be kept on plants till November 5th if desired. Has a good stout stem and clean, healthy foliage. A good shipping variety of easy culture, every stem producing a perfect

Ethelyn.

No collection is complete without F. J. Taggart.

flower. Average height, 5 ft.; second crown or terminal bud. One of the very best early commercial yellows ever offered. Certificate C. S. A. 40c ea.; $4.00 per doz.; $25.00 per 100.

Mdlle. Marie Liger.—(Hill Importation.) This is the new French variety that won the prize offered by the Chrysanthemum Society of America, for the finest seedling at the recent Paris Exposition. It also was certificated by all the committees of the Society this year. It is one of the grandest varieties of recent years and will rank with Robinson, Appleton and Eaton in popularity, because it has all the requisites to make it indispensable. Closely incurving blooms of large size. The color is pearl pink, deepening to a very bright shade at the base of petals. In habit it is dwarf, June planting only reaching three feet in height. Late propagations require no stakes or tying. Stems are stiff and fully covered with handsome foliage. It is perfectly uniform, perfecting every flower. Date of blooming is October 20th and later; best from second crown. A great variety for bush plants in pots. Shade lightly for best color.

Miss Stella T. Elkins.—(Michell.) This variety has shown up well and was greatly admired wherever exhibited. A dark red Japanese Reflexed of fine finish and color. Good grower. A welcome addition to the early class, being at its best October 25th. Best red at Philadelphia not yet disseminated, and Certificate C. S. A.

Mrs. Harry V. Casey.—(Binder.) A Japanese Incurved of exceptional merits. Silvery pink; grand, when fully expanded. At its best November 5th. Sturdy, dwarf habit. Certificate C. S. A.

Mrs. Rufus W. Smith.—(May.) A clear shining white Japanese Incurved. Symetrical, without being stiff or formal. Excellent stem and foliage, with a sturdy, healthy constitution. Average size, 6½ in. in diameter by 5½ in. deep; in season, end of November. Average height, 4 ft. Best on terminal buds. One of the very best late varieties ever offered. Certificate C. S. A.

R. E. Richardson.—(Hill & Craig.) Schray's pink. The brightest, clearest pink yet introduced in the Chrysanthemum family. Both color and form are exquisite. Incurving, but loose enough

Sephia.

to show the high color of the surface. C. S. A. Certificate and Silver Medal at Chicago, best pink at Brooklyn show and Certificate of Merit at Philadelphia. Good stiff stem and perfect foliage; height, 4 to 5 ft. Start early and take first bud after Sept. 1st.

The Yellow Eaton, or Dr. Oronhyatekha.—(Hill & Craig.) A bright yellow sport from Timothy Eaton, only a shade or two lighter than Appleton, and especially valuable as the very best of its color to follow that fine variety up to the close of the Chrysanthemum season. It has the perfect habits of Eaton, but lacks the coarseness sometimes attributed to that variety. For everybody's use and commercial purposes, as well as for show, we can cheerfully recommend this new variety; it is strictly A1. Use second crown bud. Certificate C. S. A.

Uwanta.—(May.) Bold, well built flower of good substance, and in color, a beautiful shade of amaranth. Free, vigorous grower, coming in just right for Thanksgiving, when nearly all other deep-colored varieties are passed. Height, 4½ ft.; diameter, 6 to 6½ in. Either bud. C. S. A. Certificate. 40c ea.; $4.00 per doz.; $25.00 per 100.

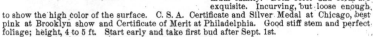

We would be pleased to furnish you a list of Chrysanthemums, giving height and season of flowering, if it will assist you in making your selection. Always state type preferred. Also, if for exhibition or commercial use.

Foreign Novelties.

We have never had the pleasure to offer such a fine lot of foreigners. From England and Australia, we have enormous Japanese blooms, ranging in color from pure white to deep purple and crimson, while many of those from France are decided improvements on the Carnot and Morel type. The Japanese Incurved section has also been strengthened by the addition of several superb varieties. Your collection is incomplete, if it does not include some of these. The following list contains many that were in winning classes this season.

Crown buds are recommended for most of these varieties, although some latitude should be given in this respect, owing to our climatic conditions, which are entirely different from those of foreign countries. Bear in mind that crown buds, as a rule, give lighter colored, more double and longer stemmed flowers than the later buds.

Price, 50c ea.; $5.00 per doz., except where noted. Ready March 1st.

Bessie Godfrey.—Deep cream or canary yellow. Very similar to Mme. Von Andre in form, but larger and fuller. Dwarf habit.

Brumaire.—An enormous incurving Japanese flower, with very broad channeled petals. Color, rosy lilac with silvery reverse; grand in form. One of the most striking for collections.

Calvat's Sun.—An enormous Japanese Incurved. Color, golden yellow; long broad petals. One of the largest blooms extant. Received four first-class certificates in France, scoring 98 points, 25c ea.; $2.50 per doz.

Chas. Longley.—Deep rosy purple Japanese. Large flowers, with long, broad florets, some drooping, others incurving. Distinct and good.

C. J. Salter.—An immense Japanese Incurved variety of fine build and good habits. Color, bright, clear yellow. Very prominent at several of the eastern shows, where it was pronounced a rival to Appleton.

Depute Baragiola.—A very curious and striking flower of immense size. In color, a fine shade of red and yellow. Petals horizontal and tubular, making an enormous spread. This ought to be in every collection. 35c ea.; $3.50 per doz.

Durban's Pride.—A monster Japanese. Color, lovely bright mauve pink, quite distinct; a full 8 in. flower and of easy culture. This variety should please exhibitors.

Edward VII.—A very large, claret crimson flower. A robust, easy grower, producing very full flowers with broad petals, slightly curling and incurving at the tips. Extremely massive.

H. W. Buckbee.

Florence Molyneaux.—This variety was very conspicuous at several of the late exhibitions. An extra large broad-petaled white Japanese of fine finish. It is of easy culture and

Remember we allow 5 per cent. discount for CASH.

good habit. When fully developed, it very much resembles Timothy Eaton, but unlike that variety it is pure white.

G. H. Kerslake, Jr.—Pearl white Japanese of dwarf habit. A handsome flower, sure to become a favorite exhibition variety.

Godfrey's King.—Reddish crimson with bright gold reverse. A splendid flower, in shape resembling M. Chenon de Leche. Long florets of medium width.

Guy Hamilton.—Large, pure white flowers, outer petals gracefully reflexing, center loosely incurved. An improved Nellie Pockett, being larger and of better color. Dwarf habit.

Lady Roberts.—Beautiful deep crimson, with bright gold reverse and tips. Winner of the Gold Medal in Melbourne for the best new sort.

N. B. Entirely distinct from "Lady Roberts" sent out by The F. R. Pierson Co., in 1900, which is pure white and similar to Timothy Eaton.

Louis Leroux.—Color, clear nankeen shading to pale pink. One of the prettiest combinations that we have seen, reminding one of the beautiful old sort called Incandescent. Petals large, center incurving and the outer ones reflexing. A fine grower with beautiful foliage. Equally good for commercial use or exhibitions. 35c ea.; $3.50 per doz.

Louis Leveque.—A fine red flower of large size, good form and well filled with petals. A nice dwarf grower, with extra fine foliage up to the flower. A perfect variety from every standpoint. Received two first-class certificates abroad.

Miss Minnie Bailey.

Mabel Manwarring.—Long, drooping and curling florets, something like Edith Pilkington; color, deepest yellow. A large 8 in. flower, of good growth and habits; 5 ft. high. 75c ea.

Mabel Morgan.—A Japanese Reflexed bloom of large size. Bright, clear yellow, destined to become one of the best of its color.

Matthew Smith.—Golden yellow ground, heavily spangled with crimson. A very easy grower. The largest bloom at several shows last fall.

Meredith.—Deep rosy terra cotta with buff reverse; similar in color to M. Chenon de Leche. The florets are an inch broad, loosely incurving, forming an enormous bloom full to the center. Large foliage and stiff stem. Good grower.

Mdlle. Marg. Douillet.—One of the finest whites yet introduced; pure in color and exquisite in form. Immense blooms, slightly reflexing. Belongs to the Carnot family, but has a stiff stem and good foliage. A fine commercial and exhibition variety. 35c ea.; $3.50 per doz.

Miss Daisy Moore.—A very distinct sort of great substance. Reflexed, outer petals twisted; full to the center; color, bright pink. A splendid grower and should be in every collection.

Miss Lucy Evans.—A beautiful heliotrope pink, clearer in color and larger in size than the very popular Mrs. Coombes. Opens free and easy, having incurved center and reflexing outer petals.

M. Chambry.—An enormous Japanese of a very bright yellow color. Large, incurving petals, forming an immense ball. A vigorous grower with beautiful foliage.

Mr. F. S. Vallis.—An immense Japanese flower; yellow, deepening to a fine citron shade. Long twisting petals, reflexing into a broad, deep bloom as large as Mme. Carnot. Far superior to that variety, being easier to grow.

Mme. Ch. Diederiechs.—A large Japanese variety. Creamy white, with center canary color on opening, but gradually becoming a beautiful shade of cream. Long, slightly reflex-

Always give complete shipping directions, plainly written.

ing petals, with incurving center. Belongs to the Carnot type, but unlike that variety, it has a good stiff stem, fine foliage and short neck. 35c ea.; $3.50 per doz.

Mme. E. Nicoullaud.—Beautifully rounded incurving form; large and deep. Broad petals regularly arranged. Color, milky white with creamy center. Fine for exhibition and general purposes. 35c ea.; $3.50 per doz.

Mme. L. Chevrant.—A rosette shaped flower of large size, having straight overlapping, pointed petals. The color is exquisite, being pure rose pink with touches of salmon; not a disagreeable shade in it. A nice, easy grower, with good stem and foliage. This should be grown in quantity another year.

Mme. G. Bruant.—An enormous exhibition variety. Color, bright rose shaded white. Has shown up well at several exhibitions. 25c ea.; $2.50 per doz.

Mme. Herrewege.—A pure white sport from Australie. Large, incurved bloom of fine finish. Easy grower.

Mme. Jean Seince.—From second crown this brings creamy white blooms tinted rose. Long petals cut at the tips and reflexing. A sport from the fine variety Mme. Ricoud, which scored 93 points last year in France.

Mme. Paolo Radaelli.—A prize winning variety, both in Europe and America. Has attained an enviable position wherever grown. The habit, foliage, neck and stem are all good. A fine grower and an easy doer. Color, creamy white, delicately flushed with rose. A deep, incurving, rounded flower with broad, whorling petals, the outer ones reflexing. Beautiful as well as curious. First or second crown. 35c ea.; $3.50 per doz.

Mme. R. Cadbury.—An exceedingly fine creamy white Japanese. Immense, deep flowers with broad, graceful petals; center loosely incurved. Good grower. 35c ea.; $3.50 per doz.

Mme. Von Andre.—(Yellow Mutual Friend.) A light yellow sport from Mutual Friend, identical except in color. As a show variety, it is unexcelled.

Mrs. Alexander McKinley.—Terra cotta. A beautiful, drooping flower, 7 in. either way. Splendid dwarf, sturdy habit; 4 ft. high. Distinct from everything else. 75c ea.

Mrs. C. J. Salter.—Lovely crimson scarlet, with drooping florets. This should not be too highly fed in its early stages, then nothing can surpass it in color. 75c ea.

Millicent Richardson.—A massive

Mrs. J. J. Mitchell.

flower; purple claret, with silvery reverse. Free, easy grower. A grand exhibition variety.

Mrs. T. W. Pockett.—Deep canary yellow. Long, rather narrow reflexing florets. The most lovely flower it is possible to imagine; more refined than Nellie Pockett. Equal in size to Yellow Carnot, but better in color and growth. 75c ea.

Mrs. J. C. Neville.—An immense white Japanese of great substance, being 10 in. across and of proportionate depth. Wide, drooping florets, forked and incurving at tips. As shown in this country, it was pronounced much better than Mrs. Weeks. 75c ea.

Mrs. Harry Emmerton.—An immense Carnot seedling of fine yellow color and grand reflexing form. Splendid exhibition variety with flowers that rival the parent in size and beauty. Robust constitution.

Mrs. R. Darby.—A Japanese variety of large size. Color, purple amaranth. Long, drooping florets, center incurving. Dwarf habit; early November.

Strengthen your collection with our Foreign Novelties.

Queen Alexandra.—Delicate buff, shaded rosy pink. A very unique and charming flower of large size. Good habits.

Quo Vadis.—A large, broad-petaled, closely incurving Japanese; rosy crimson, reverse pale gold. This variety has all the good qualities of a fine exhibition sort.

Robert Laird.—A beautiful dwarf white, reflexing after the style of Nellie Pockett. Fine for exhibition.

Silver Queen.—A handsome shade of pink; incurving form. A splendid flower, every bloom coming good.

T. Humphreys.—Deep chestnut. A splendid reflexing variety, 7½ in. in diameter. This is one of the most distinct and pleasing varieties yet introduced. 75c ea.

Vicar of Leatherhead.—This magnificent variety is a seedling from Mme. Carnot. Immense blooms, of golden yellow color. Long petals, gracefully drooping and curling. 35c ea.; $3.50 per doz.

W. R. Church.—Crimson maroon, with bluish steel reverse. Large, incurved blooms of great depth. A good grower of dwarf habit. Will become a leading exhibition variety.

Aside from the above, we have many other meritorious foreign varieties, but in too small a quantity to catalogue.

If in need, send us a list of your wants and we will quote as far as possible.

Novelties of 1902.

10c each; $6.00 per 100, except where noted.

Adrian.—This is a closely incurved creamy white Japanese. When grown cool, it has a tendency to come light pink. High, rounded flowers of good size. Owing to ease of culture and quick growth, it is a very desirable variety for the commercial grower.

A. J. Balfour.—This beautiful variety has taken a prominent place among pinks, owing to its attractive color, which is a lovely shade of bright rose. Very large, broad-petaled Japanese blooms, very much resembling Perrin in form and color. Its dwarf, short-jointed growth makes it especially desirable as a commercial variety. As an exhibition bloom, it has won many prizes. It does not make many cuttings until early spring, therefore cannot promise in quantity until the middle of April. 15c ea.; $10.00 per 100.

Bentley.—In color, it very much resembles Autumn Glory, being clear pink, with salmon shadings on the younger petals. A fine, high built Japanese, averaging 7 in. in diameter when well grown. Heavy foliage and stiff stem; height 3 to 4 ft.; early mid-season.

Calvat's '99.—A very large Japanese, with broad, incurving petals. Delicate pearl, flushed with pink. Excellent stem and foliage. A grand exhibition variety of beautiful finish.

C. Holst.—Large white Japanese of globular form, resembling Marie Louise in every way. Stiff stem, well clothed with foliage. In perfection a few days earlier than Robinson. Good keeper and shipper. 5c ea.; $4.00 per 100.

Colette.—An enormous Japanese Incurved of fine form and finish. Very double, closely incurved blooms; white, lower petals shaded lilac. Dwarf habit; early mid-season. This is a very effective variety for collections.

Cremo.—A light yellow sport from Glory of Pacific, and an exact counterpart in everything except color. No grower of the parent should be without this. 5c ea.; $4.00 per 100.

Earl of Arran.—Long, drooping petals, slightly incurving at the tips. Color, a lovely shade of bright canary yellow, deeper at the center. It is of dwarf habit and easy culture. Good for exhibition or commercial blooms. 5c ea.; $4.00 per 100.

Edgar Sanders.—As anticipated, this has taken its place among the best exhibition varieties. It is of large size, artistic form, and dark bronze in color. Broad, incurving petals, forming a compact bloom. One of the easiest varieties to grow. Best from terminals. Crown buds produce larger flowers, but have tubular guards and are reflexed in form. Height, 4½ ft.; size, 7½ in.

Geo. Carpenter.—A first-class exhibition bloom, owing to its color, which is light rosy

---

A. J. Balfour is an improved Perrin.

amaranth. Long petaled, high built Japanese blooms of large size. Heavy foliage and stem. Height, 4 ft.; developed Nov. 1st; good from either bud.

Harry A. Fee.—The most distinct and striking of any variety recently sent out. Closely reflexed blooms of medium size. Color, chestnut red, with the end of each petal distinctly tipped with yellow. As each petal hooks up slightly at the end, the effect is very pleasing. Height, 3 ft. Best from terminals. 10c ea.; $8.00 per 100.

Henry Stowe.—Large, deep Japanese bloom of good substance. Color, light rose pink, often white from early crowns. Broad petals, loosely incurving at center. A good exhibition variety.

Honesty.—Immense, white Japanese blooms. The outer petals are tubular and reflexed. The center consists of strap petals loosely incurving, making a flower of great depth; 8 in. in diameter. Dwarf, robust habit; early mid-season.

James Parker.—A large, creamy white Japanese. Flat, spreading flower. Dwarf habit; healthy grower.

Kansas City Star.—Resembles Nagoya in height and general habits, also size, form and substance. In color, it is a beautiful shade of light pink; very pleasing, especially under artificial light. A first-class commercial variety; at its best Nov. 15th to 20th. Terminal bud.

Lily Mountford.—This cannot be too highly recommended, as it has all the characteristics of a first-class variety. Immense Japanese blooms 8 in. in diameter, very double and of good substance. Color, light rose, the center changing to creamy white at maturity. Height, 3 ft.; best from second crown. Stem and foliage similar to that of Morel. It is inclined to bud during the winter months, and we are therefore unable to furnish in quantity until early spring. 15c ea.; $12.00 per 100.

Lizzie Adrock.—A deep yellow sport from Source d'Or, very useful for decorative work. Small Japanese flowers of wonderful texture. Best grown in bush form; medium height. 5c ea.; $4.00 per 100.

Marian Newell.—A broad-petaled reflexed variety, double to the center. The flower when fully developed, measures 9 in. in diameter. The color is almost pure pink, without the magenta so often seen in pinks. A fine exhibition variety, although inclined to be late. Crown bud only.

Edgar Sanders.

Mdlle. Renee Aiotte.—The best early bronze to date, being 7 in. in diameter and fully developed Oct. 25th. Color, true bronze; lower petals reflexed, center slightly incurved. Dwarf, sturdy growth, with heavy foliage, making it especially valuable for commercial use.

Mira.—Drooping and incurving petals loosely arranged. Delicate rose, lighter at the center. Very rigid stem; dwarf. 10c ea.; $8.00 per 100.

Miss Jessie Cottee.—This is a golden yellow sport from Etoile de Lyon, and as this makes a very large bloom, the sport will be a valuable addition to the exhibition class.

Miss Lullah Miranda.—A variety that should be more extensively grown, as it combines size with ease of culture. A large, high built Japanese; very broad, pure white petals. Briefly described as an enlarged Niveus. Height, 3 ft.; at its best Nov. 10th.

Do not forget Yellow Eaton and Marie Liger when ordering.

Mme. Gabrielle Debrie.—Pale flush pink. Long, drooping petals, curling and incurving at the tips. A first-class exhibition bloom in every way.

Mme. Phillipe Roger.—A very large Japanese Incurved bloom, having very broad, slightly hirsute petals. Color, dark bronze, with lighter reverse. At its best Nov. 1st to 5th. A useful bronze for early exhibitions.

Mme. V. Claverin.—A light purple Japanese of large size. Its form, size and color, all tend to make this a grand exhibition variety.

Mrs. F. J. Taggart.—A seedling from Golden Wedding by Goldmine, having the stiff stem and fine foliage of the former, and the size and deep yellow color of the latter. Ray florets tubular, center is strap petals. Fine for late shows. Free, healthy grower. 10c ea.; $8.00 per 100.

Mrs. Geo. Mileham.—Long, broad florets, gracefully drooping, with loosely incurved center. Color, silvery mauve, with deeper shadings. A large, finely shaped variety of great merit. It has made a great showing at several exhibitions, and similar reports come from England. 10c ea.; $8.00 per 100.

Mrs. Greenfield.—A loosely arranged globular bloom. Broad petals; color, rich golden yellow. Stiff stem, with foliage close under the flower; either bud. We predict a future for it as a commercial variety. It is larger than Robert Halliday and flowers at the same time.

Mrs. J. F. Trantor.—Enormous, reflexed blooms of great depth. Color, white, penciled rose pink, giving the bloom a decided pink cast; good habits. An exhibition variety of exceptional merits.

Mrs. Wm. Fraser.—This variety has shown many points of excellence, such as size, form, dwarf habit and ease of culture. A large, broad-petaled Japanese Reflexed bloom; in color, bright crimson lake, which makes it a very desirable exhibition variety. Early mid-season. Good stem and foliage. 10c ea.; $8.00 per 100.

Opah.—This is the best commercial variety sent out last season, and one that has taken the place of Lady Fitzwigram wherever grown. It very much resembles this variety in form, but is stronger in growth and readily makes a 6 in. flower on a stiff stem with common culture. First flowers cut this season were fully developed Oct. 1st, and the last Oct. 15th. Color, pure white from crown. Terminals are a beautiful shade of blush pink. Is not subject to the disease so prevalent among Fitzwigram early in the season.

Oresco.—A Jones seedling, having same foliage and habit. In color, it is a beautiful apricot, shaded rose, changing to crushed strawberry when fully matured. It is double to the center and larger than Mrs. Jones. Distinct and novel. It is a fine seller owing to its attractive color.

Polar Queen.—A very large, pure white Japanese of good substance. Stem and foliage A1 in every respect, being the finest of any Chrysanthemum in our stock. Outer petals reflexed, center irregularly incurved, making a graceful, high-built flower. Take terminal bud only. At its best Nov. 30th; height, 3 ft. A first-class commercial variety.

Pride of Elstowe.—An early mid-season pink of pleasing tint. A seedling from Mrs. E. G. Hill. Large flowers on very stiff stems, well clothed with foliage. Dwarf habit. Good for commercial use.

Princess Alice de Monaco.—Large, spreading, pure white flowers of fine finish and texture. The petals are slightly incurved at the tips. Free, easy grower.

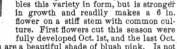
Mrs. F. J. Taggart.

For a good, extra early white, try Opah.

Prosperity.—This is a welcome addition to the Incurved class. Very double, ball shaped blooms, 4 in. in diameter. Pure white on crowns and blush on terminals. Its habits are all that could be desired. 5c ea.; $4.00 per 100.

Providence.—Disseminated last season as a sport from **Western King**, but growth and form of flower do not resemble it. However, it is a fine variety, very similar to Belle of Castlewood in every particular except color, which is light nankeen yellow. Distinct and pretty.

Rev. Douglas.—Large, deeply built flower, with drooping florets; in color, pure yellow. Perfect growth. This is another promising commercial and exhibition variety. Height, 3 ft.; 6 in. in diameter; early mid-season.

Sirius.—Pure white Japanese Reflexed, with excellent stem and foliage. Dwarf, sturdy habit. Very desirable for pot culture. 5c ea.; $4.00 per 100.

Southern Cross.—A rich, brilliant yellow Japanese Incurved variety with incurving and twisting florets of good substance. The blooms are well carried on stiff stems. Very late.

Swanley Giant.—Large, massive incurved flowers. Color, lilac pink with lighter reverse. Height, 3 ft.; good grower.

T. D. M. Cardeza.—Rich, golden yellow, reflexed flowers on strong, stiff stems, heavily clothed with deep green foliage.

Ville de Bordeaux.—A Japanese variety with broad, blush pink petals. An immense, showy flower. Very good stem and foliage. Extra fine for exhibition or cutting.

W. H. Whitehouse.—A magnificent flower; in form similar to Morel, but has longer petals. Color, a distinct shade of rosy lilac, striped white. Excellent grower.

Opah.

HOW TO GROW CHRYSANTHEMUMS.

A COMPLETE TREATISE ON THE SUCCESSFUL CULTURE OF THE QUEEN OF AUTUMN.

We are sorry to inform our patrons, that it will be impossible for us to furnish the above work, as advertised last season.

However, the publishers are enlarging the former edition and revising it to date, to embrace the latest methods of culture.

This work will be completed and ready for distribution during March at an advanced price of 50 cents per copy, post-paid, NET.

Pompon Novelties of 1902.

10c each; $6.00 per 100.

Alena.—A flat, reflexed flower; ends of petals notched. Beautiful Daybreak pink; 3 ft.
Daze.—Dahlia-like petals. Light rose. Extra fine grown in sprays, or disbudded; 3 ft.
Elko.—Small, globular, compact blooms; magenta; 2 ft. Fine for bush culture.
Lero.—Small flowering; very free. Deep lilac, shading to magenta; 3 ft.
Livan.—Perfect, solid blooms; white, edged pink. Sprays or disbudded; 4 ft.
Orea.—Deep rose, with lighter shadings. Perfect, globular flowers, 3½ in. in diameter when disbudded. Dahlia-like petals. A beautiful and valuable addition to the class.
Tulu.—A small flowered variety of most perfect form. Blush white; 3 ft. high.
Utan.—Light magenta, edged and tipped white; fine globular form; very attractive; 3 ft.

General Collection.

Early.

5c each; $3.00 per 100, except where noted.

Polar Queen.

Geo. S. Conover.—A large, early yellow variety. Splendid habit and stem.

Geo. S. Kalb.—Pure white; style of Bergman, but larger; very double; dwarf habit.

Glory of Pacific.—A leader among early pinks. Dwarf, sturdy growth.

H. L. Sunderbruch.—A grand, early yellow bush plant variety. 5c ea.; $4.00 per 100.

Ivory.—Pure white, globular formed flower. The most extensively grown white.

J. E. Lager.—Very large reflexed yellow. Exceedingly strong grower.

John K. Shaw.—A commercial pink of incurving form. One of the best of its color.

Lady Fitzwigram.—A well-known extra early white of dwarf habit. 5c ea.; $4.00 per 100.

Lady Harriett.—A deep pink Japanese Incurved variety of dwarf growth. 5c ea.; $4.00 per 100.

Lady Playfair.—Large, globular flowers. A good second early pink of easy culture.

Marquis de Montemort.—The earliest pink to date. Moderately tall.

Marion Henderson.—A very good, large early yellow of reflexed form. An easy doer.

Merula.—A dwarf Japanese Incurved of a beautiful shade of light pink. Good single stem variety.

Polar Queen as a dwarf, late white has few equals.

Midge.—The best dwarf, early white. Resembles Bergman, but is an improvement in every way. Beautiful stem and foliage.

Mme. F. Bergman.—A very popular early white, which is still grown by many.

Mme. Gastellier.—(Syn. Independence.) Creamy, changing to pure white; Bergman form.

Monrovia.—A bright yellow, early Japanese variety, having the form of Bergman, but much larger. Stiff stem, well clothed with foliage; medium height. The best early yellow on the market.

Mons. Benj. Giroud.—The best early crimson. Very dwarf. 5c ea.; $4.00 per 100.

Mrs. E. G. Hill.—A very large Japanese Incurved, of a pleasing shade of pink. Good grower.

Omega.—The largest early yellow in commerce. In form, similar to Morel; 7½ in. in diameter; at its best, Oct. 25th. It is giving universal satisfaction. 10c ea.; $6.00 per 100.

Pink Ivory. — (Syn. Agnes L. Dalskov.) The well-known pink sport from Ivory.

Polly Rose.—A pure white sport from Glory of Pacific. Very popular.

Pride.—A large white Japanese, flowering with Marion Henderson. Very Good.

Primo.—A clear white Japanese variety of large size. Perfect habits; very early.

Robert Halliday.—A large, broad-petaled Japanese flower with perfect stem and foliage. Dwarf habit. One of the finest second early yellows.

Soleil d'Octobre.—(October Sunshine.) A yellow Japanese of good substance and excellent habits, flowering a few days later than Rob't Halliday. Heavy, short-jointed growth.

Walter Molatsch.—Very fine second early yellow Japanese Incurved of large size and good substance. Dwarf, sturdy habit. An effective early exhibition variety.

Willowbrook.—An early Japanese variety of good substance. Fine grower. Very popular.

Yellow Fitzwigram.—A yellow sport from Lady Fitzwigram. 5c ea.; $4.00 per 100.

Omega.

Midseason.

5c each; $3.00 per 100, except where noted.

Admiral Dewey.—A large Japanese Reflexed. Deep chrome yellow, similar to Thornden.

A. H. Fewkes.—A very dwarf, bright yellow Japanese. Fine growth. 10c ea.; $6.00 per 100.

Autumn Glory.—A large Japanese flower on the style of Morel. Soft shrimp pink color.

Black Hawk.—Dark, crimson scarlet; style of Morel. An extra fine red for all purposes.

Boule d'Or.—A very large incurving flower; color, golden buff. Dwarf habit.

Brutus.—A large, handsome flower; very bright red, shaded with orange. Ideal growth. One of the best for bush or specimen plants. 10c ea.; $6.00 per 100.

Bruant.—A reddish bronze Japanese Incurved of large size. One of the best of its color for exhibitions.

Buff Globe.—A sport from Good Gracious. Buff, shaded orange.

Captain Gridley.—A high built Japanese Incurved of large size. White, shaded blush.

Our stock of Standard Chrysanthemums includes many varieties not listed. Write us if in need of such.

We have the popular varieties in quantity. When you are ready to plant, let us make our best terms.

Casco.—Japanese Incurved. A distinct shade of dark garnet. Very dwarf. 5c ea.; $4.00 per 100.

Chestnut Hill.—An excellent variety for pot culture. Clear, bright yellow, of excellent form and substance. Heavy, short-jointed growth. 5c ea.; $4.00 per 100.

Chito.—Strap petal; fine red stripes on yellow ground, giving a bronzy appearance.

Chas. Davis.—A light bronze sport from Morel. 5c ea.; $4.00 per 100.

Col. D. Appleton.—Large, golden yellow Japanese Incurved. The most popular of its color.

Curly Locks.

Curly Locks.—A very artistic bloom, often 12 in. in diameter. A loosely incurved Japanese, outer petals tubular. Color, a beautiful pink, changing to white at center.

Elmer D. Smith.—A very large, broad petaled Japanese. Cardinal red.

Eureka.—Porcelain white; size and form similar to Philadelphia. Good habits; height, 4 ft. 10c ea.; $6.00 per 100.

F. A. Spaulding.—A bright yellow sport from Mayflower.

Frank Hardy.—A pure white sport from Good Gracious. Take crown bud only.

G. J. Warren.—(Syn. Yellow Mme. Carnot.) A yellow sport from Mme. Carnot. 5c ea.; $4.00 per 100.

Gen. Antonio Maceo.—A seedling from John Shrimpton, being of the same color, but does not sunburn or fade. Exceedingly dwarf. The best crimson for pot culture. 5c ea.; $4.00 per 100.

Geo. W. Childs.—An exquisite shade of bright crimson. The best crimson with many. Give high cultivation until buds are formed and do not feed thereafter. 5c ea.; $4.00 per 100.

Gold Standard.—Immense blooms; form, color and style of Golden Wedding.

Golden Shower.—One of the most distinct and unique Chrysanthemums. Long, drooping, hair-like florets, interlacing like corn silk. Yellow, intermingled with bronze and red petals; very dwarf. Makes beautiful specimens.

Golden Wedding.—One of the best standard yellows. 5c ea.; $4.00 per 100.

Good Gracious.—Soft pink; quilled petals irregularly incurved.

Helen Bloodgood.—True, clear pink of an exquisite shade. Rather tall.

Henry Weeks.—An immense, broad-petaled Japanese; rosy crimson. Exhibition.

Hicks Arnold.—Golden bronze; incurving form; makes fine bush plants.

H. J. Jones.—One of the largest crimsons to date, the average diameter being 8 in. Reflexed, on style of Morel and just as double. A winner at many shows. 15c ea.; $10.00 per 100.

Hon. W. F. D. Smith.—A very large, brilliant crimson Japanese with good stem and foliage. 5c ea.; $4.00 per 100.

Idavan.—A large, compact bloom of the Mrs. Robinson type. Delicate pink, center creamy.

Iora.—An exceedingly artistic flower of light pink color. Petals tubular their entire length, incurving in a whirl. Successfully shown last fall. 5c ea.; $4.00 per 100.

Jeannie Falconer.—(Syn. Peter Kay.) A very large, lemon yellow exhibition flower. 5c ea.; $4.00 per 100.

John Shrimpton.—A well-known crimson; fine for pots. 5c ea.; $4.00 per 100.

Kate Broomhead.—A very large flower, of a pleasing shade of golden amber. Fine grower. A winner in the bronze class. 10c ea.; $6.00 per 100.

Lady Anglesey.—A true, dark bronze sport from Chas. Davis; an improvement in every way. 5c ea.; $4.00 per 100.

Lady Hanham.—Cerise pink, shaded with gold. A sport from Morel. Beautiful pink under artificial light. 5c ea.; $4.00 per 100.

Omega—the largest early yellow in commerce.

Lillian B. Bird.—Straight tubular petals pointing in every direction; soft pink. A very novel and pretty flower. 5c ea.; $4.00 per 100.

Malcolm Lamond.—A very dwarf red, same color as Fisher's Torch, but an improvement. Good dwarf grower; does not sunburn. 10c ea.; $6.00 per 100.

Marie Calvat.—A delicate pink Japanese of dwarf habit. A valuable exhibition variety.

Mary Hill.—Habit, growth and form of Perrin, of which it is a seedling. Light shade of pink, pearl reverse. A good commercial variety.

May Foster.—This is one of the best for bush plants. Flowers resemble a small Ivory both in color and form. Has heavier foliage than Ivory and of the same height.

M. B. Verlot.—A long, broad-petaled Japanese Incurved of large size. Color, rose mauve. One of the largest of this type, and a valuable addition to the exhibition class. 5c ea.; $4.00 per 100.

Major Bonnaffon.—Very soft, clear yellow of perfect Incurved form and dwarf habit.

Marg. Jeffords.—A large, incurving bronze bloom. Very popular in some places.

M. Chenon de Leche.—A Japanese flower of large size. Color, amber and yellow. Sturdy growth. None better for exhibitions. 10c ea.; $8.00 per 100.

Merza.—An extra large, pure white Japanese Incurved of dwarf habit. Perfect stem and foliage. As a single stem variety it has no equal, and has outclassed many of our prominent whites at the shows. It has also received premiums as the largest bloom at several exhibitions last fall. 10c ea.; $6.00 per 100.

Minnie Wanamaker.—A pure white Japanese Incurved. An old standby.

Miss Alice Byron.—Among the many varieties recently introduced from Europe, this variety has shown exceptional merits as a commercial white, being an easy doer and pure in color. Broad, incurving petals similar to Mrs. Weeks. It also resembles it in growth, but flowers with Mrs. Robinson. Makes an effective exhibition bloom either in vases or in pots. 10c ea.; $6.00 per 100.

Miss Georgiana Pitcher.—A bright yellow Japanese Incurved of perfect form. Robust, but short jointed growth, with foliage set close to the flower. Crown bud only.

Miss Florence Pulfman.—Large, loosely arranged white Japanese. Fine form.

Mme. Carnot.—Very large, pure white Japanese. Although an old variety, there are few that can equal it as an exhibition flower when well grown. 5c ea.; $4.00 per 100.

Mme. F. Perrin.—An extra fine globular flower of a pleasing shade of bright pink.

Modesto.—Rich yellow Japanese Incurved of large size. Still one of the best of its color.

Mrs. Ritson.—A beautiful white sport from Morel. 15c ea.; $10.00 per 100.

Mrs. F. A Constable.—A pure white sport from Iora. 5c ea.; $4.00 per 100.

Mrs. Barkley.—A very large, broad petaled Japanese of dwarf, sturdy habit. Color, rosy mauve, with silvery reverse. It has been successfully exhibited in many localities. No collection should be without it. 10c ea.; $6.00 per 100.

Mrs. J. J. Glessner.—A distinctive formed light yellow, lower petals shaded apricot. Excellent keeping qualities.

Mrs. M. A. Ryerson.—A pure white Japanese of artistic form. Narrow petals, reflexed from crown bud and irregularly incurved from terminal. Fine for exhibitions.

Mrs. Elmer D. Smith.—An immense deep golden yellow Japanese Incurved of perfect form. It is brighter in color than Golden Wedding or Appleton. Perfect stem and large foliage; seldom exceeds 3 ft. in height. Exceptionally well adapted for a single stem pot plant, as it needs no support. Avoid heavy top dressings and do not feed after buds are formed. No grower should be without this fine variety, as it embraces all the desirable characteristics of an ideal chrysanthemum. 5c ea.; $4.00 per 100.

Mrs. H. Weeks.—A very broad petaled pure white Japanese Incurved; perfect stem and foliage. It has been winner in vase, single stem and bush plant classes. On several occasions it has won over the great Timothy Eaton.

Mrs. S. C. Probin.—Pure pink Japanese Incurved with silvery reverse. Excellent dwarf habit. 5c ea.; $4.00 per 100.

Mrs. Coombes.—This is another foreigner which has gained prominence, both as a commercial and exhibition variety. An enormous reflexed flower with very broad petals; in color, a beautiful shade of light rose. The chief attraction is its dwarf, short jointed growth and heavy foliage. Fine for pots, either as a bush or single stem plant. It possesses excellent keeping qualities. Superior to Morel in every way, and we predict it will be the standard second early pink of the future. 10c ea.; $6.00 per 100.

Mrs. W. Mease.—A sulphur yellow sport from Mme. Carnot. 5c ea.; $4.00 per 100.

A discount of 5 per cent. is allowed on all orders with CASH.

Mrs. A. J. Drexel.—Bright crimson lake Japanese. Still the best of its color for show purposes. 5c ea.; $4.00 per 100.

Mrs. J. Peabody.—A very large, pure white exhibition Japanese, of fine form and finish.

Mrs. Geo. A. Magee.—A Japanese Incurved of perfect globular form and large size. Rosy lilac.

Mrs. W. B. Chamberlain.—An exhibition bloom of large size. Outer petals drooping, center incurving; color, a lovely shade of pink; very heavy stem and foliage.

Mrs. W. C. Egan.—A very large Japanese Incurved, with excellent stem and foliage. Color, creamy white, suffused with pink. Extra fine for early exhibitions.

Mrs. H. Robinson.—A large, pure white Japanese Incurved. Good for all purposes.

Mrs. O. P. Bassett.—A light yellow sport from Mrs. H. Robinson.

Mutual Friend.—A broad, spreading flower of the purest white. Owing to its dwarf habit it is especially adapted for single stem and bush plants. As an exhibition bloom, it has few equals. 5c ea.; $4.00 per 100.

Nellie Pockett.—Large, creamy white Japanese with long, drooping florets curling at the tips. Strong, compact growth. Equally valuable as a commercial or exhibition bloom. It is being extensively grown in this country. Best from crown bud. 5c ea.; $4.00 per 100.

Neseta.—A Japanese of large size. Long, broad strap petals, loosely arranged. Color, light yellow; dwarf, sturdy, short-jointed growth.

Niveus.—Grand white of easy culture. Valuable for all purposes. Can be flowered late.

Nyanza.—Broad-petaled Japanese Incurved; crimson, with golden reverse. 5c ea.; $4.00 per 100.

Orizaba.—A large Japanese Incurved, of a pleasing shade of light pink. Dwarf, sturdy habit and of easy culture. Perfect stem and foliage. None better for single stem plant. One of the best standard pink varieties. 5c ea.; $4.00 per 100.

Pennsylvania.—A bright yellow sport from Pennsylvania. 5c ea.; $4.00 per 100.

Peter Kay.—(Syn. Jeannie Falconer.)

Petaluma.—A very distinct and attractive flower of large size. Quilled petals, thickly set, forming a globular bloom often 9 in. in diameter. In color, a very even shade of light bronze. 5c ea.; $4.00 per 100.

Philadelphia.—Japanese Incurved; whorled center. Creamy white, tipped primrose. 5c ea.; $4.00 per 100.

Pitcher & Manda.—Tubular petals. Inner portion of the flower yellow, while the outer five or six rows of petals are white. Very unique.

Red Warrior.—A large Japanese; color, chestnut red. Makes a beautiful bush plant.

Rustique.—A bold, closely incurved flower of the largest size. In color, a distinct shade of golden brown. Good grower. A sure winner at the exhibitions. 5c ea.; $4.00 per 100.

Shilowa.—A very artistic, brilliant crimson Japanese, of easy culture and good habits.

Silver Cloud.—Delicate salmon pink. A Japanese exhibition flower of fine form.

Silver Wedding.—A large, pure white, reflexed flower of good substance. Very broad petals.

Simplicity.—A pure white Japanese variety equal to Mme. Carnot in size.

Sunstone.—Style of the Queen. Bright yellow, shading to red at base; light straw reverse.

Timothy Eaton.—An immense Japanese Incurved bloom of easy culture and good habits. Pure white when matured. The most popular of its color at the present time.

T. Carrington.—An Australian that has outclassed many of our best exhibition varieties. Enormous Japanese Incurved bloom of fine form and texture. Color, rich carmine rose, with silvery reverse; second crown or terminal. Good stem and foliage. Makes an elegant bush plant.

The Queen.—A very popular white Japanese Incurved.

Thornden.—A bright yellow Japanese of large size; very good. Feed sparingly.

Vivian Morel.—Immense bright pink Japanese. A favorite with many. 5c ea.; $4.00 per 100.

Walleroo.—Very broad-petaled blooms, slightly incurving on the style of Niveus. Color, rosy cerise. A fine exhibition variety, especially for collections.

Western King.—A pure white Japanese Incurved; strong grower. Can be had very late from late cuttings. One of the finest whites. 10c ea.; $6.00 per 100.

Yanariva.—Another welcome addition to the pink class. A blush pink Japanese on the style of Morel and of the same size. It is of easy culture and has remarkable keeping qualities.

Let us submit a list of best exhibition sorts.

Yellow Mayflower.—A lemon yellow sport from Mayflower.
Yellow Mme. Carnot.—(Syn. G. J. Warren.)
Zulinda.—A large flower, of glossy finish and good substance. Color, silvery rose; outer petals tubular, slightly reflexing; center incurving. Exhibition only.

Late.

5c each; $3.00 per 100, except where noted.

Clara Goodman.—A very good reflexed flower on the color and style of **H. W. Rieman.**
Eclipse '98·.—A light yellow sport from Wm. H. Chadwick. 5c ea.; $4.00 per 100.
Golden Beauty.—(See syn. Mrs. E. Buettner.)
Goldmine.—An immense bloom; outer petals reflexed and center incurving in a whirl. Color, rich golden yellow. The best for late shows and Thanksgiving Day sales. 5c ea.; $4.00 per 100.
Harry Balsley.—Unequaled among pinks. Plant late and feed generously; terminal bud.
Henry Nanz.—A bronzy yellow sport from Mrs. J. Jones.
H. W. Rieman.—Fine, high rounded flower of bright yellow color; dwarf. 5c ea.; $4.00 per 100.
Intensity.—A large reflexed flower, showing only the bright crimson upper surface of petal. Strong, upright growth. It has no equal as a late commercial exhibition red.
Invincible.—A large, incurving white, sometimes tinted pink. A very desirable variety.
Lavender Queen.—A pleasing shade of light lavender pink. Outer petals reflexed and center erect, making a flower of great depth. Very heavy foliage and stem. The largest and finest of its color for late shows and Thanksgiving sales.
Maud Dean.—Beautiful rose pink; still grown by many. 5c ea.; $4.00 per 100.
Mdlle. Lucie Faure.—A pure white, closely incurved flower of perfect form; good habits.
Merry Christmas.—Large, flat flower. The latest white. 5c ea.; $4.00 per 100.
Mrs. E. Buettner.—(Syn. Golden Beauty.) After several trials, we find that Golden Beauty, recently sent out, is the old variety Mrs. E. Buettner, disseminated in '96 by Emil Buettner. Although old, it can be classed among our best late yellows. 5c ea.; $4.00 per 100.
Mrs. Geo. F. Baer.—(Syn. Yellow Mrs. J. Jones.)
Mrs. S. T. Murdock.—Soft pink; excellent stem and foliage. A favorite bush variety.
Mrs. J. Jones.—A very popular pure white, grown by many. Good keeper.
Nagoya.—Very large Japanese blooms, same color as Modesto. Large, heavy stem and foliage. It is of easy culture and ranks among the best Thanksgiving yellows.
Superba.—Very double, high built flower, similar to Maud Dean, having the same upright growth and foliage, but is perfectly double. Color, bright pink. Take terminal bud only. The best and most profitable Christmas flowering variety. 5c ea.; $4.00 per 100.
V. H. Hallock.—A beautiful Japanese of good substance. Color, beautiful light rose.
White Bonnaffon.—In form, identical with Bonnaffon, and general habits same as Robinson. Color, pure ivory white. A valuable Thanksgiving variety.
W. H. Lincoln.—Bright yellow. A well-known variety.
Wm. H. Chadwick.—An immense white Japanese, center loosely incurving. Occasionally striped pink from late bud. The largest and best late mid-season white, both commercially and for exhibition purposes.
Xeno.—A closely incurved variety, having the dwarf habit, good stem and foliage of Perrin, but perfectly double. Color, light rose like Maud Dean. An ideal Thanksgiving pink. Terminal bud only.
Yanoma.—A very late, loosely arranged pure white flower. One of the best.
Yellow Mrs. J. Jones.—A bright yellow sport from Mrs. J. Jones.

Anemone Section.

10c each; $6.00 per 100.

Ada Strickland.—Light chestnut red; full and high center; broad ray petals.
Condor.—Very large; tubular rays; rosy purple, tipped yellow.
Descartes.—Bright crimson red rays and cushion; dwarf habit; extra.

Late Chrysanthemums pay best.
Try GOLDMINE, SUPERBA and CHADWICK.

Enterprise.—Ray florets light rose; sulphur yellow center. Fine form.
Eulalie.—Pure white broad-petaled flowers of medium size. Center sometimes shaded yellow.
Falcon.—White rays, shaded pink; pale, straw yellow center. Medium size.
Garza.—Single row of broad ray petals; well formed center. White, tipped yellow. It is especially adapted for bush plants, being the center of attraction when well grown.
James Weston.—White ray petals; lemon yellow center. Small flower.
John Bunyan.—Lemon yellow; long, fluted guard petals; darker center.
Junon.—Blush pink, extra large and dense cushion.
Marcia Jones.—Immense snow white flowers of perfect form. Rich cushioned center.
Mrs. F. G. Dexter.—Double row of white rays; rose pink center. Very large.
Mrs. Hugh Gardner.—Deep rose; high disk, tipped gold.
Queen Elizabeth.—Silvery blush; long ray florets; center tipped yellow.
San Joaquin.—Lemon yellow center, pure white guard. One of the best.
Satisfactio.—Chrome yellow, suffused with gold and amber. Trumpet-like florets.
Sir Walter Raleigh.—Pale blush guards, deeper colored cushion. Exceedingly pretty and effective.
Surprise.—Forked and hooked guard petals; high center; pink florets. The best.
Thorpe Jr.—Pure golden yellow. Extensively used as an exhibition flower.
W. W. Astor.—Long, flat guard petals. Pure white; high golden center.
Zoraida.—A very large, artistic flower. White ray florets; pure yellow center.

Hairy Section.

10c each; $6.00 per 100.

F. J. Taggart.—(For description and price, see novelties.)
Golden Hair.—Bright chrome yellow, suffused with amber. Densely covered with spines.
Improved Louis Boehmer.—A light pink sport from Louis Boehmer.
L'Enfant des deaux Mondes.—Pure white sport from Louis Boehmer.
Leocadie Gentils.—A bright yellow sport from L'Enfant des deaux Mondes.
Louis Boehmer.—Magenta pink. This and its sports are excellent for bush culture.
Mrs. C. B. Freeman.—A bronzy yellow sport from Louis Boehmer.
Mrs. Higinbotham.—A large, bright pink flower. Extremely wide petals.
Pluma.—One of the most perfect of its type; color, very delicate pink.
Queen of Plumes.—A beautiful shade of bright pink. Very full and of fine form.
R. M. Grey.—(Syn. Hairy Wonder.) Terra cotta. One of the most distinct and best.
White Swan.—A closely incurved pure white flower, very heavily plumed.
Yellow Louis Boehmer.—(See Leocadie Gentils.)

Incurved Section.

Owing to the limited call for varieties of this class, we have discontinued the propagation of same. However, we have a good collection in stock and will propagate any of the varieties on demand.

Pompons.

All Pompons are suitable for bush plants. They are of the easiest culture, require very little training and yield flowers in abundance. For small specimens, the dwarf varieties are most suitable. There is an increasing heavy demand for cut flowers, either in sprays or disbudded. The following list contains the best for all purposes, and no progressive florist should be without at least part of them:

5c each; $3.00 per 100.

Acto.—Incurving; dahlia-like petals. Bright rose with lighter reverse; 2½ ft. high.
Aileen.—Deep lilac pink, close compact form and of medium size. Very neat and pretty.
Angelique.—Pure white, high built flower; very compact and graceful.
Black Douglas.—Rich dark crimson; perfect form. The best of its color.

Anemone and Hairy varieties are very artistic and beautiful.

Delicatissima.—Lower petals Daybreak Carnation color; center deep wine.
Gallia.—Clear soft pink when fully developed. Excellent form. Good for any purpose.
Garda.—A small flowering pure white; dwarf. Very desirable for small pot plants.
Jeanevieve.—Blush pink; large flower. Extra fine variety.
Julia.—Color, deep crushed strawberry red; fringed edges. Distinct and striking.
Klondike.—Compact bloom of medium size; brilliant yellow. Very useful.
Lula.—Pure snow white bloom of medium size. Of easy culture and very free. Rather late.
Magnificus.—Pure white flowers of large size and extra good form. Very beautiful.
May Williamson.—White, changing to pink when developed. Large and perfect in form.
Mdlle. Martha.—Fine dwarf white; good habits.
Miss Ada Williams.—White, shaded blush and sometimes laced with violet. Very useful.
Mrs. Bateman.—Orange brown; large. One of the best of its color.
Nita.—Beautiful rose pink; extra fine, full double flower of the large flowering type.
Novia.—Delicate pink; Daybreak Carnation color. Very perfect form; early.
Nydia.—Pure white, high rounded flower; fine form; large flowering. Late October; 3½ ft.
Quinola.—Clear orange yellow, of excellent form and good size. One of the best.
Snowdrop.—Pure white; small flowers; very profuse bloomer.
Vera.—White, slightly flushed pink; large flowering. Dahlia-like petals. Height, 2½ ft.
Viola.—Deep violet. A very showy and distinct flower.
Yezo.—Small flowering; very perfect. Ball shaped; 1 in. in diameter. Blush; 2 ft.
Zenobia.—Bright clear yellow of a brilliant shade. Handsome flower. Fine in sprays.
Zenta.—Bright crimson maroon; full double flower of perfect form; 2½ ft. high.

Pompon Anemone Section.

5c each; $3.00 per 100.

Aglaia.—Blush, changing to white; large.
Antonious.—Golden yellow guard florets and disk. Rather large; dwarf.
Emily Rowbottom.—Blush white sport from Marie Stuart.
Firefly.—Bright scarlet with high center. A very distinct and striking color.
Mme. Chalonge.—Blush guard florets; blush, shaded to sulphur disk.
Mme. Sentir.—Pure white; beautiful high center.
Norma.—Ray petals, deep bronze. Clear yellow center.
Reine des Anemones.—Pure white; very fine.
Rose Marguerite.—Deep rose. Very strong grower.

Early Hardy Pompon Section.

5c each; $3.00 per 100.

Bronze Bride.—Rosy bronze sport from Blushing Bride.
Frederick Marronet.—Orange, striped red.
Illustration.—White, shading to pink.
Mdlle. Elsie Dordan.—Soft lilac pink; very neat, full globular bloom; dwarf.
Mr. Selley.—Rosy lilac; dwarf, compact habit and very free.
Piercey's Seedling.—Orange bronze, changing to bright yellow with age. Dwarf, sturdy habit.
St. Mary.—Pure white. Fine.

Note the many useful Pompons we offer.

Single Section.

5c each; $4.00 per 100.

Mizpah.—Daisy-like flowers; color, bright rose; height 12 to 16 inches. As a decorative variety, it has no equal. Owing to its dwarf habit and freedom of bloom, it is exceedingly desirable as a border or bush plant.

The following varieties are seedlings from Mizpah, having the same general character and form of flower, but of different color:

Argenta.—Pure white.
Rosina.—Light rose pink.
Zeroff.—Bronzy yellow when developing, changing to pure yellow at maturity.

Carnation Novelties for 1903.

30c each; $3.00 per doz.; $12.00 per 100, except where noted.

Prices quoted are for STRONG, WELL ROOTED CUTTINGS. Not less than six at dozen, and 50 at 100 rate.

Adonis.—(Hill & Craig.) Without doubt the finest Carnation yet produced. It is the largest among reds. In color, it surpasses all, being deep, brilliant scarlet, a shade so often admired in Geraniums. Quite distinct in form, having no surplus petals, allowing the calyx to become perfect under all conditions. Stiff, erect stem, averaging 2 ft. and over in height. A free, compact grower, with no superfluous grass. It has won many medals, both gold and silver, also numerous other honors. 30c ea.; $3.00 per doz.; $14.00 per 100.

Enchantress.—(Thompson Carnation Co.) The Queen of Carnations. Just what the florists are looking for, a light pink Lawson. It is larger in size and longer stemmed. A beautiful shade of light pink, deepening toward the center; far superior to Daybreak at its very best. Immense, attractive flowers, of fine form and exceptional keeping qualities. Perfect non-bursting calyx. Both out of doors and in the house, the growth is ideal; very healthy, vigorous constitution. A free, early and continuous bloomer. Thrives in a temperature of 50 to 52 degrees. Has conquered at all the fall shows.

Gov. Lowndes.—(Weber.) A pure white of good size, averaging 3 to 3½ in. in diameter. The lower guard petals stand out straight, retaining the full size of the bloom. Slightly serrated petals, beautifully arrranged, forming a full rounded center. Calyx spreads at the top, making it practically non-bursting. Strong stem, 2 to 2½ ft. in length, carrying the flower erect at all times. Very sweet and particularly pleasing odor. Of vigorous habit and rapid growth. An early, free and continuous bloomer. More productive than any other large white. A profitable, high grade, commercial variety. 25c ea.; $2.50 per doz.; $12.00 per 100.

Harlowarden.—(Chicago Carnation Co.) The bright crimson of the future, and largest of its color, every flower being 3½ in. in diameter. Extremely long stems, 4 ft. in length and stiff enough to carry the bloom perfectly erect. In habit it is perfection, growing 4½ ft. high and straight as a bunch of wire rose stakes. The calyx never bursts. A wonderfully free bloomer, will produce at least 50% more than Gov. Roosevelt. Created a great sensation at the shows of 1902, winning many honors.

Her Majesty.—(Chicago Carnation Co.) Wonderfully productive. This is one of its chief points of merit. Pure glistening white. In form it is simply perfect. Very large blooms, on extra strong stems about 30 in. long. It is bound to become the standard white, both for winter and summer blooming, as it will commence July 1st and continue until the same time a year later. The calyx never splits and the blooms always come perfect. The greatest honor won by Her Majesty was last winter at Chicago, winning out over all the other colors, and receiving the prize for the best vase in the show. 20c ea.; $2.00 per doz.; $10.00 per 100.

Mrs. Theodore Roosevelt.—(Ward.) Color, a brilliant shade of cerise pink, with a scarlet tinge at the center. It is so brilliant that it is taken for a scarlet under electric light. Large, symmetrical flowers of great substance. Strong, well formed calyx. The petals stand well out from the calyx, thus avoiding all chance of bursting. Rigid, 2 ft. stem, holding the flower erect. Growth is first-class in every respect and not affected by any fungus disease.

Adonis, the Scarlet Carnation of the Future.

Healthy, vigorous constitution. Under same treatment and bench space, it will produce one-third more blooms than Lawson, with stems 6 in. longer.

Sibyl.—(Dorner.) A clear, cerise pink of an exceptionally bright, even color. Average size, 3 in. Form is rounding and of good depth. The arrangement of petals is perfect, very attractive, showing off the color to the best advantage, either as an individual flower or in bunch. Strong, straight stem 2 to 2½ ft. long. Every break develops a strong shoot and perfect flower. Perfect calyx; sweet fragrance. An extremely free and continuous bloomer throughout the entire season. Exceptionally good keeping qualities. As a commercial variety of its color, it will rank among the best, owing to many superior characteristics.

Those desiring larger quantities will be quoted lowest prices on application.

General Collection.

5c each; 40c per doz.; $2.00 per 100; $15.00 per 1000, except where noted.
Six at dozen; 50 at 100; 250 at 1000 rate.

Apollo.—Clear, brilliant geranium scarlet, producing large blooms, borne on stiff stems at all times. We consider it one of the best high grade scarlets. 10c ea.; $1.00 per doz.; $6.00 per 100; $50.00 per 1000.

Bon Homme Richard.—Absolutely the most profitable white carnation extant. The only white that is perfect, commercially speaking, the year round. Never stops blooming and never bursts.

Cressbrook.—Bright pink flowers, 3½ in. in diameter; stem strong and wiry. Habit similar to Lawson, and no surplus grass or foliage. Never bursts. 10c ea.; 75c per doz.; $5.00 per 100; $40.00 per 1,000.

Dorothy Whitney.—Deep yellow ground, slightly striped with pink. Large, well formed flowers, on long stiff stems. A free, continuous bloomer and of strong constitution. The best commercial yellow. 10c ea.; $1.00 per doz.; $6.00 per 100; $50.00 per 1,000.

Estelle.—In color, the most brilliant scarlet. Large, well shaped blooms. A clean, healthy, grower. Splendid keeper and shipper. One of the best commercial varieties of its color and always in demand.. 10c ea.; 60c per doz.; $4.00 per 100; $30.00 per 1,000.

Ethel Crocker.—Bright rose pink. Its freedom of bloom, extra large flowers and strong growth, make it a profitable carnation. Very free. As a summer flowering variety it has no equal.

Gaiety.—Variegated scarlet and white. Early, free and continuous bloomer. The most profitable and satisfactory variety of its color. It makes no surplus grass. The flowers are not as large as Bradt, but being less crowded with petals, it comes to perfection in about half the time. 10c ea.; 75c per doz.; $5.00 per 100; $40.00 per 1,000.

G. H. Crane.—The favorite scarlet Carnation and grown by many.

Glacier.—Pure white. An early and prolific bloomer. Excellent for design work, owing to its large size and pure color.

Gov. Roosevelt.—Rich, deep crimson. Large, well formed flowers, on stiff stems. It never bursts its calyx and is perfect in form. The favorite of its color. 5c ea.; 50c per doz.; $3.00 per 100; $25.00 per 1,000.

Lorna.—This is a decided improvement over White Cloud. Its exceptional healthy growth and productiveness will prove its value to every grower. 5c ea.; 50c per doz.; $3.00 per 100; $25.00 per 1,000.

Morning Glory.—An improvement on Daybreak, being more constant in color and giving more flowers throughout the season, without any tendency to crop.

Mrs. F. Jooste.—A beautiful shade of true rose pink. Very productive and early. 5c ea.; 30c per doz.; $1.50 per 100; $12.50 per 1,000.

Mrs. Higinbotham.—Light salmon pink, similar to a good colored flower of Daybreak. Uniform in color at all times. Strong, erect stems, with large flowers having perfect non-bursting calyx. A vigorous, free grower. Very good substance. The best of its color. 10c ea.; 75c per doz.; $5.00 per 100; $45.00 per 1,000.

Mrs. Thos. W. Lawson.—Color, clear cerise; strong, vigorous growth. This grand Carnation heads the list in standard varieties. 5c ea.; 50c per doz.; $3.00 per 100; $25.00 per 1,000.

Norway.—Pure white flowers of large size. A very vigorous, healthy grower, and does not crop. A commercial white of exceptional merit.

Enchantress conquered them all.

Prosperity.—The largest Carnation to date, but considering its enormous size, it is a free early bloomer, and the best paying Carnation where fancy blooms are in demand. Color, white ground, overlaid and mottled with pink. 5c ea.; 50c per doz.; $3.00 per 100; $25.00 per 1,000.

Queen Louise.—Pure white. It has much to recommend it as a commercial variety. Its freedom of bloom, ease of culture and perfect calyx, are among its leading features. Always in bloom; every shoot producing a perfect bloom. 5c ea.; 50c per doz.; $3.00 per 100; $25.00 per 1,000.

The Marquis.—A soft, rich shade of true pink, with no trace of purple or magenta. Large perfect flowers on long stems; very fragrant. One of the finest pink Carnations.

White Cloud.—Large well-built flowers on long, stiff stems. Color, pure white. Very free bloomer; strong, healthy growth. A standard commercial white.

Cannas.

The Express.—This is one of our productions and foremost among last year's novelties. Another year's trial has convinced us that it possesses superior merits—equaled by few, and second to none. In color it is bright scarlet crimson, a shade lighter than that of Philadelphia, one of its parents. Large, broad-petaled flowers in immense, compact trusses. The bed is a mass of bloom the entire season. Under most favorable conditions it only attains a height of 3 ft., but generally 2 to 2½ ft. This, added to its free, clean growth, makes it an ideal crimson bedder.

Strong, dormant roots, having not less than two eyes, 35c ea.; $3.00 per doz.; $20.00 per 100.

Recent Introductions.

35c each; $3.00 per doz., except where noted.

Cherokee.—Broad petals, soft and fine as velvet; rich dark maroon. Large erect trusses, borne well above the foliage. A vigorous grower, always in bloom; 3 ft. high. 10c ea.; 85c per doz.; $6.00 per 100.

Elisabeth Hoss.—Enormous trusses of spotted blooms on the style of Florence Vaughan, but much larger and richer in color. Free flowering and does not sunburn. The best spotted Canna. 15c ea.; $1.50 per doz.

Frau Bremermann.—Growth, form and color of flower, very similar to that of Sam Trelease, but stronger. Rich scarlet, often banded yellow. Free flowering.

Hermann Fischer.—Exceedingly dark purple foliage. Medium sized flowers, color, true burnt orange; strong grower. Height, 3½ ft. Best of its color.

Hofgartendirektor Walther.—A very promising dark foliaged variety. Large trusses of dark scarlet flowers, set well above the foliage. Height, 3 ft.; stools freely.

Homarschall von St. Paul.—Enormous four-petaled flowers; color, bright scarlet, similar to that of Chicago. Large green foliage on heavy foot-stalks, 4 ft. in height. The largest flower among Crozy type of Cannas.

J. Colette Rochaine.—Immense well branched trusses of large, deep orange scarlet flowers. Large musa-like foliage on heavy stem; 4½ ft. high. A very fine bedder, owing to its free flowering habit. 25c ea.; $2.50 per doz.; $15.00 per 100.

James H. Veitch.—Medium to large four-petaled flowers, loosely arranged, forming a

During the months of **AUGUST, SEPTEMBER** and **OCTOBER** we will have a large stock of field-grown **CARNATIONS**, both in Novelties and Standard Varieties.

We will also have field-grown clumps of **VIOLETS, ASPARAGUS SPRENGERII, VINCA** and the best varieties of **CHRYSANTHEMUMS.**

Write for prices when in need.

truss of immense size. Color, clear deep crimson; rich purple foliage. One of the best dark leaved Cannas known to us. An attractive bedder; height, 3½ ft.

M. Ph. Rivoire.—In growth and general habit identical with Sam Trelease. Bright scarlet, with light yellow, crimson spotted center. Very large; height, 3 ft.

Pres. Meyer.—Large four-petaled flowers and upright branching trusses. It often has two perfect heads of flowers on one stalk at the same time. Purple leaves and veins; very rapid grower; height 3½ ft. The best dark leaved scarlet Canna known to us. 15c ea.; $1.50 per doz.; $10.00 per 100.

West Grove.—An exceedingly strong, vigorous grower. Large erect trusses, nicely placed above the foliage. Well shaped flowers of remarkable substance; color, rich coral pink, dappled bright crimson at the throat. Very free. 10c ea.; 85c per doz.; $6.00 per 100.

General Collection.

10c each; 60c per doz.; $4.00 per 100, except where noted.

Prices quoted are for Strong, Dormant Roots. After April 1st, established plants only, furnished at an advance of 30c per doz.; $2.00 per 100, on prices quoted. Not less than 6 at doz.; 25 at 100, and 250 at 1000 rate.

Allemania.—Orchid flowering; the largest of this type. Outer petals dark orange, with a very broad, golden yellow border; height, 4 ft. 5c ea.; 40c per doz.; $2.50 per 100.

Annie Laurie.—A charming and lovely variety, bearing large spikes of flowers, rivaling the finest Gladiolas in color, which is exquisite silvery rose, with a distinct white throat. Very beautiful; 2½ ft. high. 10c ea.; 85c per doz.; $6.00 per 100.

Beaute Poitevine.—Rich, bright crimson flowers, on erect spikes, 3½ ft. high. Very free bloomer. One of the best bedders.

Black Beauty.—By far the darkest and most handsome colored foliage of any Canna. Unequaled for center of groups; 5 to 7 ft. high. 20c ea.; $2.00 per doz.; $12.00 per 100.

Burbank.—A beautiful clear yellow of the largest size; Orchid flowering. Medium height and free flowering. The flowers are mostly semi-double. 5c ea.; 40c per doz.; $2.50 per 100.

C. Drevet.—Very strong grower, with large green foliage. Extra large flowers; in color very similar to Mrs. Kate Gray. Free, continuous bloomer. 10c ea.; 85c per doz.; $6.00 per 100.

Chas. Henderson.—Large, handsome spikes of dark, rich crimson flowers. A standard sort and favorite in its color; height, 3½ ft. 5c ea.; 40c per doz.; $2.50 per 100; $20.00 per 1000.

Chas. Molin.—Extra large flower, composed of pear-shaped petals; flesh color with darker veins at the center and a narrow margin of light yellow. Striking and effective. 10c ea.; 85c per doz.; $6.00 per 100.

Chicago.—Large trusses of bright scarlet flowers. One of the best of its color, being an exceedingly free bloomer. Height, 4 ft.

Crimson Bedder.—Compact growth; height, 3 ft. Large trusses of well opened florets; color, bright crimson. Very early and free bloomer. 10c ea.; 75c per doz.; $5.00 per 100.

Cuba.—(Augusta.) Very large florets; intense scarlet, widely bordered with bright, clear yellow. Height, 3 ft. One of the largest gilt edged varieties. 10c ea.; 75c per doz.

Depute Ravarin.—Strong grower. Large, branching trusses. Color, bright crimson, same as Chas. Henderson, but more free flowering. 5c ea.; 40c per doz.; $2.50 per 100.

Egandale.—Deep bronze foliage. Bright crimson; 3 to 4 ft. high. Unsurpassed for bedding, owing to its rapid growth and branching habit.

Explorateur Crampbell.—Large, well filled spikes of cardinal red flowers. Height, 4 ft. One of the most valuable of its color.

Florence Vaughan.—Rich, golden yellow, thickly spotted with red. One of the finest variegated varieties. 5c ea.; 50c per doz.; $3.00 per 100; $25.00 per 1000.

Giant Crimson.—Height, 5 to 6 ft. Color, intense glowing crimson. Very vigorous growth. An excellent bedder. 10c ea.; 75c per doz.

Canna "The Express" is the finest dwarf crimson. A bed of it will always be a mass of bloom.

Golden Bedder.—What is said of Crimson Bedder, applies to this variety, except that it is more dwarf in habit, attaining a height of 2½ ft; also has small florets. Bright golden yellow with a faint trace of red at base of petals. Very free and early. 10c ea.; 75c per doz.; $5.00 per 100.

Leonard Vaughan.—Fine dwarf bronze variety of splendid habit. Large trusses of bright orange flowers. One of the finest dark leaved varieties. 10c ea.; 85c per doz.; $6.00 per 100.

Leopard.—Extremely stalky grower; height, 4 ft. Large compact trusses of bright canary flowers, broadly blotched and spotted with rich crimson. Free and distinct.

Martha Washington.—Very large, broad petaled flowers in well filled trusses. Color, pure, bright rose; height, 3 ft. Our best pink Canna. 10c ea.; 85c per doz.; $6.00 per 100.

Mdlle. Berat.—Fine bright pink flowers in large, well filled heads; long, gracefully drooping petals. Very free flowering; height, 4 ft.

Mme. Alfred Blanc.—Very heavy flower stalks; height 3 ft. Large trusses of medium sized flowers; broad, rounding petals. Color, deep salmon with yellow shadings. Very good. 10c ea.; 85c per doz.; $6.00 per 100.

Mme. Louis Druz.—Broad, rounded petals, forming a round flower very similar to Sam Trelease. Fine, compact flower heads; color, bright scarlet; does not sunburn. Very free; height, 3 ft. 10c ea.; 75c per doz.; $5.00 per 100.

Mrs. Kate Gray.—Immense, bright scarlet flowers, which do not burn in the hottest weather. The spikes very often branch, making five and six trusses. Very strong, musa-like growth, with large, bronzy green foliage; height, 6 ft. A hybrid between the orchid flowering and Crozy type. 15c ea.; $1.50 per doz.; $10.00 per 100.

Pennsylvania.—In growth and general habit it resembles Mrs. Kate Gray, but darker in color and only five feet high. Unsurpassed as a bedder. 20c ea.; $2.00 per doz.; $12.00 per 100; $100.00 per 1000.

Philadelphia.—Very intense scarlet crimson. Dwarf and vigorous, with flowers from 5 to 6 inches across. It is an early and continuous bloomer. A leader in its color.

Pierson's Premier.—Rich crimson scarlet, mottled and edged with yellow. Handsome trusses of large, bold flowers. A fine bedding variety. 10c ea.; 60c per doz.; $4.00 per 100; $35.00 per 1000.

Pres. Cleveland.—Fine, large flowers, in heavy erect trusses. Bright orange scarlet; height, 3 ft. A popular bedder.

Pres. McKinley.—Color, fiery crimson scarlet. An early, constant and profuse bloomer. Dwarf habit, fine foliage, stools freely and is very valuable for pot culture, single specimen, or massing.

Queen Charlotte.—Rich crimson, with a broad margin of yellow. Although old, it is still considered one of the best of its color. 5c ea.; 50c per doz.; $3.00 per 100.

Robusta.—Large, bright bronze foliage, unequalled for tropical effect. With good cultivation, will grow fully 10 ft. high. 5c ea.; 50c per doz.

Rosemawr.—Bright rosy pink, mottled with dark rose. Extra large flowers, having broad, rounded petals. Very showy and handsome. 15c ea.; $1.25 per doz.; $8.00 per 100.

Souv. de Mme. Crozy.—Bright scarlet, bordered with rich golden yellow. Height 3 ft. One of the showiest of the gild-edged class.

Mixed Cannas.

We have a large lot of these in separate colors, scarlet and crimson, variegated or spotted, and pink. Also mixed named varieties, and seedling tubers, raised from the very best home grown seed, of about 40 standard sorts.

Those desiring a mixed bed, will be more than pleased with our stock.

Unnamed, separate colors, 40c per doz.; $2.00 per 100.

All colors, mixed; 25c per doz.; $1.50 per 100; $10.00 per 1000.

Try Canna Pennsylvania. It is the best of the Orchid-flowering section.

Geraniums.

Novelty for 1903.

Double Dryden.—(Eichholz.) A double form of Dryden. No florist, knowing the value of this popular variety, can afford to be without the double form. 35c ea.; $3.00 per doz.

Tom Thumb Section.

10c each; $5.00 per 100, except where noted.

America.—A Mars seedling, having the same dwarf habit and freedom of bloom but much stronger in growth. Blush white, changing to pure rose pink when fully matured. An ideal pot and bedding Geranium.

Dr. E. A. Hering.—Single. Brilliant scarlet, overlaid with crimson. Dwarf, compact growth. As a free continuous bloomer, it has no equal.

Eben E. Rexford.—A counterpart of above in every way except color, which is brilliant pink with white eye. Both are very useful and attractive bedders.

Little Pink.—The finest double pink of the Mars family. Does not exceed 6 in. in height, making an ideal pot variety. Strong, compact growth. The illustration shows its free flowering nature.

Mars.—Brilliant salmon pink at center, shading to white at margin. It is a very dwarf, free bloomer, the plants being entirely covered with medium sized trusses of single blooms. Must be seen to be appreciated.

Little Pink.

Merle Blanc.—(New.) A valuable addition to this section, being a very dwarf, pure white, double variety. An excellent bedder, the plants being a mass of white the entire season. The flowers are not large, but every branch of the plant produces a truss. 15c ea.; $1.50 per doz.

General Collection.

5c each; $3.00 per 100, except where noted. Not less than 5 at 100 rate.

Dryden.—Single bedder. Lower petals scarlet, upper petals white, bordered scarlet. Dwarf, compact growth and very free. Is not easily affected by dry weather. 5c ea.; $4.00 per 100.

Duc de Montemart.—Velvety carmine. Dwarf and exceedingly free flowering. Very large double florets. This is one of the best bedders we have.

Emanuel Arene.—Very large double florets. Pure white, with broad bands of rosy scarlet making a flower of rare beauty. Extremely vigorous grower.

Hubert Charron.—Semi-double blooms, clear white center with a broad band of reddish carmine around each petal. As a bedder it has no equal, being a good grower and exceedingly free.

Carefully read Terms of Sale on second page of cover.

J. J. Harrison.—Rich, brilliant scarlet of the Bruant type. Immense flowers, many measuring over 2 in. in diameter.

Jean Viaud.—Semi-double Bruant. Color, a beautiful shade of bright rose, which does not fade in the hottest weather. Extra strong growth and large foliage. Without exception the best pink bedder.

La Favorite.—Double white. A favorite bedding and market variety.

Le Gaulois.—(New.) Very large, intense scarlet in fine large trusses; splendid bloomer. Clean, free grower; perfect bedder and worth thorough trial. 10c ea.; $5.00 per 100.

Le Soleil.—(New.) One of the best double scarlet bedding Geraniums yet introduced. A most profuse bloomer and stands the sun well. Color, brilliant scarlet; very intense in masses. Healthy, robust growth; immense trusses. 10c ea.; $6.00 per 100.

Marie Fournier.—Large, semi-double blooms; deep, brilliant rose pink, with distinct white eye. The individual floret is exceptionally large and profusely borne in large trusses. Very vigorous, dwarf habit.

Marquis de Castellane.—(New.) One of the most distinct and beautiful of the recent introductions in the Bruant section. Large trusses of well shaped large flowers profusely produced. The color varies from brilliant cerise to cherry red, often shaded carmine. Strong, vigorous habit. Will rank with Jean Viaud and others of this class. 10c ea.; $6.00 per 100.

Marvel.—Double crimson bedder. Grown by many in place of S. A. Nutt.

Mme. Barney.—(New.) A splendid pure deep pink. Truss, habit and profuseness of bloom, all that can be desired. Stands wet weather best of 'all in this class; a magnificent variety. 10c ea.; $5.00 per 100.

Mme. Charotte.—Distinct pure salmon, occasionally veined with white. Semi-double Bruant. Extra large trusses, with individual florets 2 in. and over in diameter. A decided improvement on Beaute Poitevine both in color and growth.

Mme. Jaulin.—Bruant type. Delicate pink, bordered with pure white. Entirely distinct in color. A very popular bedder.

Mme. Landry.—Semi-double Bruant. Fine dwarf 'habit and an exceedingly profuse bloomer. Deep apricot salmon, darker than Beaute Poitevine. The best bedder of its color, and a worthy companion to Jean Viaud.

Mme. Buchner.—Double white. More vigorous in constitution than La Favorite, and preferred by many.

Precurseur.—(New.) A large, pure white single Bruant, occasionally tinted flesh in the old flower. A fine grower and very free. Valuable for bedding, and the first white of its class. 15c ea.; $1.50 per doz.

Richelieu.—A valuable variety in the double crimson section, being the strongest grower in this class. Large trusses of deep crimson maroon florets.

Robert Charlie.—(New.) Semi-double Bruant. Beautiful rosy mauve, several shades darker than Eben E. Rexford. Large flowers of perfect form. Blooms continually. 15c ea.; $1.50 per doz.

Sam Sloan.—Light crimson, single bedder. Large trusses, abundantly produced the entire season.

S. A. Nutt.—The best and most popular double crimson to date.

Theodore Theulier.—Single. Brilliant vermillion scarlet. Very free flowering and one of the best bedding varieties.

Double Ivy Leaved Section.

5c ea.; 50c per doz., except where noted.

From a large list of varieties, we have selected the following, which are considered the best both from color and cultural standpoint:

Flourens.—Shell pink, with satin lustre.

Jeanne d'Arc.—Pure white, extra.

La Rosiere.—Delicate rose pink.

Leopard.—(New.) Absolutely distinct from any other variety. Large, semi-double florets. Ground color, clear lilac, upper petals blotched deep crimson and heavily dotted maroon. Very attractive. 15c ea.; $1.50 per doz.

Souv. de Chas. Turner.—Deep, bright pink.

Mme. Salleroi.—Variegated green and white. The most popular border plant. 5c ea.; $2.50 per 100.

Happy Thought.—Tri-colored foliage. Single, crimson flowers. 5c ea.; 50c per doz.

Jean Viaud and S. A. Nutt are the best bedders.

Pelargoniums.

Sandiford's Nonsuch.

Price, 10c ea.; $8.00 per 100, except where noted.

Bridegroom.—A very pleasing shade of rosy blush, tinted maroon; beautifully crimped flowers. Dwarf and very free. 20c ea.; $12.00 per 100.

Crimson King.—For freedom of bloom, depth of color and good habit, we do not hesitate to predict that it will become one of the most popular varieties for market purposes. As its name implies. it is of an intense crimson color. 20c ea.; $12.00 per 100.

Evening Star.—Deep crimson, spotted and blotched. Pure white throat. Exceedingly free flowering and of easy culture. 15c ea.; $10.00 per 100.

Innocente.—A grand flower of good substance. One-half again as large as any other white Pelargonium. Beautifully frimbriated; pure white. Fine for design work. Very dwarf. 15c ea.; $10.00 per 100.

Linda.—A remarkable free flowering Pelargonium, producing large trusses of elegantly fringed flowers. Color, beautiful orange pink, upper petals feathered with maroon. A very attractive flower. 15c ea.; $10.00 per 100.

Prince George.—Enormous trusses of finely fringed white flowers, faintly suffused with blush, all the petals spotted with maroon. A very attractive flower. 15c ea.; $10.00 per 100.

Sandiford's Nonsuch.—(New.) Bright rosy crimson, edged blush white, upper petals blotched dark maroon, shaded light purple around the throat. One of the best market and decorative varieties for florists' use. As its name denotes, there are "none such" like it. It eclipses any other variety in the quantity and beautiful color of the flowers. (See illustration.) 20c ea.; $15.00 per 100.

W. C. Boyes.—Of a pleasing shade of salmon; very large and bold. Remarkably free bloomer and beautifully crimped. 20c ea.; $12.00 per 100.

Capt. Raikes.—Flowers very large and full. Color, dark fiery crimson; crisp petals of great substance. A free, easy grower.

Mrs. R. Sandiford.—The finest double white. Snow white flowers with beautifully ruffled edges.

Rob't. Green.—Extra strong, robust growth. Medium sized flowers. Color, clear rose pink, lower petals having a dark maroon blotch. 10c ea.; $6.00 per 100.

Sandiford's Best.—A beautiful shade of pink, surrounded with a broad band of white; large white throat.

Sandiford's Wonder.—Splendid semi-double pure white flowers, some showing a rich maroon spot in upper petals; heavily fringed.

Victor.—Color, bright cherry pink; white at base of petals, upper petals blotched deep crimson maroon. One of the best and a favorite with all.

Sandiford's Nonsuch is a beauty.

Nephrolepis Piersoni.

The Pierson Gold Medal Fern.

(F. R. Pierson Co.)

The most notable introduction in decorative Ferns since Adiantum Farleyense. The pinnae of the frond subdivides making perfect miniature fronds. The fronds grow broad and heavy, measuring at least 6 in. across when fully developed, increasing in beauty as they develop. They more nearly resemble the graceful ostrich plume, than anything else in nature to which we can compare them. The picture of a plant on back of catalogue gives a very good idea of the feathery, plume-like fronds, although one has to see a plant in growth to appreciate its beauty and value. On account of the weight of the foliage, the plant assumes an exceedingly graceful appearance, and, owing to the fullness of the fronds, even small plants are well furnished, making much more symmetrical and beautiful plants than the Boston Fern. The divided pinnae, or the miniature fronds, keep growing constantly, showing two distinct shades of green, the ends being a light green, while the center and main part show a dark, rich shade, the contrast producing a very beautiful effect, greatly enhancing the beauty of the plant. It is valuable, not only on account of its beauty, but also for its ease of culture, hardiness and general adaptabilty. It has all the free growing, hardy characteristics of the Boston Fern, and, like that plant, is equally suitablefor house culture and a much more beautiful plant for greenhouse and conservatory decoration. Medals, Certificates of Merit and Press Comments have been generously bestowed upon this beautiful horticultural novelty, from all parts of the country.

The demand is enormous, so place your orders early. They are filled in strict rotation, beginning in February.

Strong plants from 2¼ in. pots, $1.00 ea.; $9.00 per doz.; 50 plants at 60c ea.; 100 plants at 50c ea.

We can also supply larger plants as follows: From 4 in. pots, $2.00 ea.; $18.00 per doz. Fine large plants from 6 in. pots, $2.75 ea.; $27.00 per doz.

Acalypha Bicolor Compacta.

Acalypha Bicolor Compacta.—(Vaughan.) A most wonderful plant. It surpasses the finest Coleus or Begonia in the beautiful coloring of its leaves. Bright green ground, margined with a wide, irregular band of lemon yellow and having wide yellow bars running lengthwise of the leaf, also thickly dotted with yellow blotches. Entirely distinct from all other Acalyphas, and is a first class plant for greenhouse decorations. Its most important feature, is the wonderful qualification for bedding, as it will stand bedding out like a Coleus, in fact, the highest coloring is produced in sunny places. The leaves are large, oval-shaped, varying in size, the largest measuring 8 inches long by 4½ inches wide. Compact, free branching habit, rarely over 18 inches in height. When better known, it will become indispensable for all decorative work. Strong, well established plants, from 2½ in. pots, ready early in February. 25c ea.; $2.50 per dozen; $12.50 per 100.

Violets.

Price for strong, established plants, 5c ea.; $2.50 per 100, except where noted. Rooted runners quoted on application.

Double.

Hardy English.—Suitable for out door planting in the northern states, being very hardy. Color, dark purple, and exceedingly fragrant.

Lady Hume Campbell.—Lighter in color than Marie Louise; free grower and very productive. Does best when grown a few degrees warmer than other violets.

Marie Louise.—Large, deep blue flowers. The most extensively grown double violet.
Swanley White.—Very healthy grower. The best double white.

Single.

California.—Hardy. Very dark blue. Vigorous plant, absolutely free from disease.
La France.—An improvement on Princess of Wales, being a stronger grower, better in color and larger in size. 10c ea.; $5.00 per 100.
Princess of Wales.—Color, true violet blue; very productive. The most popular among the single violets, and one of the best for winter forcing.
White Czar.—Strong grower; very free bloomer. Best single white.

Hardy Perennials and Ornamental Grasses.

Anemone Japonica.—ALBA.—Large, single, pure white flowers. 10c ea.; $5.00 per 100.
—ELEGANTISSIMA.—Two rows of beautiful satin rose petals. Possesses an exceedingly robust constitution, and averages 5 ft. in height. A new variety of exceptional merit. 10c ea.; $5.00 per 100.
—LADY ARDILAUN.—A pure white variety with broad, over-lapping petals. An improvement over Alba. 10c ea.; $5.00 per 100.
—MONTE ROSE.—A beautiful shade of rose, reverse of petals, lilac. Large 4 in. flowers with four or five rows of petals. Another meritorious novelty. 10c ea.; $5.00 per 100.
—QUEEN CHARLOTTE.—One of the most popular varieties in cultivation. Semi-double flowers; color, a beautiful shade of light pink. Commences to bloom earlier than most varieties. 10c ea.; $5.00 per 100.
—ROSEA SUPERBA.—Light rose bloom of fine form and substance. An improvement on Elegans. 10c ea.; $5.00 per 100.
Anthemis.—KELWAYII.—A hardy Marguerite. Exceedingly free flowering, even in the poorest soil. Deep yellow. 5c ea.; $4.00 per 100.
Arundo.—DONAX VAR.—A reed-like plant, growing to a height of 6 ft., forming a dense clump. Foliage variegated, creamy white and green. Strong, dormant eyes, 20c ea.; $15.00 per 100.
—MACROPHYLLA GLAUCA.—A remarkable strong growing variety, attaining a height of 12 to 15 ft., with foliage 4 in. wide. The leaves are dark, glossy green on the upper surface and a glaucous color underneath. Strong, dormant eyes, 20c ea.; $15.00 per 100.
Aster.—TRINERVIUS.—A magnificent, perfectly hardy variety. Owing to its late flowering habit (Nov. 15th), it seldom reaches perfection in the Northern States. Large, deep blue flowers, produced in profusion. Grown in pots, it makes a valuable decorative plant, especially desirable at Chrysanthemum exhibitions. In the Central and Southern States, it comes grand planted out of doors. 5c ea.; $3.00 per 100.
Boltonia.—LATISQUAMA.—One of the showiest of our native plants. Large, single, aster-like flowers, entirely covering the plant during the summer and autumn months. 4 to 5 ft. high. Pink, slightly tinged lavender. 10c ea.; $5.00 per 100.
Caryopteris.—MASTACANTHUS.—(Blue Spirea.) A handsome half-hardy perennial plant. It is of vigorous growth, producing flowers in great profusion the whole length of its branches, even young plants in small pots flowering freely. The color is a rich lavender or sky blue. A valuable plant, either for bedding or pot culture, blooming continually from midsummer until cut by frost. 5c ea.; $4.00 per 100.
Cassia.—FALCATA.—(Half hardy.) A valuable border plant, just as useful as Salvia Splendens, especially when planted with dark leaved Cannas. Numerous clusters of curious shaped, lemon yellow flowers, completely covering the plants during August and September. Nip the plants until August 1st, and very bushy plants will be the result. 10c ea.; $6.00 per 100.
Chrysanthemum.—MAXIMUM TRIUMPH.—Large, daisy-like flowers, 3 in. and over in diameter. Pure white, with golden yellow center. Bushy plants, continuing in full bloom from early July until late October. Valuable as a cut flower, being of great substance. A rival to Shasta Daisy. 10c ea.; $5.00 per 100.
Coreopsis.—LANCEOLATA GRANDIFLORA.—A very valuable perennial, flowering from early June until late fall, producing an abundance of bright yellow, daisy-like flowers, which are exceedingly useful for decorative purposes. 5c ea.; $3.00 per 100.
Digitalis.—GLOXINIOIDES.—(Foxglove.) One of the most satisfactory of all summer flowering perennials. We offer the finest strain of the spotted throat class. Mixed colors. 5c ea.; $3.00 per 100.

Anemones give an abundance of flowers. Try our collection.

Erianthus.—RAVENNAE.—Closely resembles Pampas Grass, growing 10 ft. in height and crowned with a large silvery plume in late autumn. 10c ea.; $6.00 per 100.

Eulalia.—GRACILLIMA UNIVITTATA.—Very narrow, bright green foliage, gracefully drooping. A beautiful ornamental grass. 10c ea.; $6.00 per 100.

—JAPONICA VAR.—A graceful variety from Japan, with narrow leaves striped green and white. Flower stalks from 4 to 6 ft. high. 10c ea.; $6.00 per 100.

—JAPONICA ZEBRINA.—The long blades of this variety are marked with broad yellow bands across the leaf. Large, branching plumes. 10c ea.; $6.00 per 100.

Eupatorium.—AGERATOIDES.—(Hardy Ageratum.) A useful border plant, of strong, free growth, 3 to 4 ft. high, and producing small white flowers in dense terminal heads, from late July until frost. Exceedingly useful for floral work. 5c ea.; $4.00 per 100.

Helianthus.—MAXIMILLIANA.—A most graceful single-flowered variety, 5 to 7 ft. high. Very late flowering. Invaluable for cutting. 10c ea.; $5.00 per 100.

—MISS MELLISH.—Grows about 6 ft. high, with an abundance of large, single golden yellow flowers. Very showy. 10c ea.; $5.00 per 100.

—MOLLIS.—Large, single lemon yellow flowers, with downy white foliage; blooms in August and September; height, 4 ft. 10c ea.; $5.00 per 100.

—MULTIFLORUS PLENUS.—Large, double yellow flowers; center petals notched. The plant is entirely covered with flowers from early August until frost. 10c ea.; $5.00 per 100.

—MULTIFLORUS GRANDI-PLENUS.—(Soleil d'Or.) An improvement on the above in size, the flowers sometimes being 5 in. in diameter. Unlike the former, it has broad, dahlia-like petals. For general effect and usefulness the above has no equal. The best hardy double sunflower. 10c ea.; $5.00 per 100.

—MULTIFLORUS MAXIMUS.—A gigantic single variety, growing from 5 to 6 ft. high. Immense single, golden yellow flowers, from July to September. One of the finest. 10c ea.; $5.00 per 100.

—ORGYALIS.—A tall variety 6 ft. high, with medium sized single golden yellow flowers, during September and October. 10c ea.; $5.00 per 100.

—RIGIDUS.—One of the most desirable of the single sunflowers, both for cutting and decorative effect. 3 ft. in height. Golden yellow flowers with dark center, blooming from July to frost. 10c ea.; $5.00 per 100.

—TOMENTOSUS.—Entirely distinct, growing about 4 ft. high and producing during August and September, single, rich yellow flowers about 3 in. across. Very useful for cutting. 10c ea.; $5.00 per 100.

Helenium.—AUTUMNALE SUPERBUM.—Grows from 6 to 7 ft. high, with broad heads of deep golden yellow flowers during late summer. 10c ea.; $6.00 per 100.

—HOOPESII.—Bright, orange yellow flowers, about 2 in. across. The earliest to bloom, producing its flowers very freely from June to September on plants 3 to 4 ft. high. 10c ea.; $6.00 per 100.

Heliopsis.—SOLEIL D'OR.—The best of its class, producing throughout the summer, a mass of golden flowers. As an ornamental hardy plant it has few equals. 10c ea.; $6.00 per 100.

Lychnis.—VISCARIA SPLENDENS.—A strong, vigorous grower, making large clumps of almost evergreen foliage. Comes into bloom early in June and continues for 6 weeks or more. Semi-double, daisy-like flowers. Color, bright crimson, useful for cutting. Without doubt, the finest red flowered perennial. 10c ea.; $6.00 per 100.

Monarda.—DIDYMA.—A rapid growing plant, producing bright red flowers, at each tip; 5 to 8 in. high. Very satisfactory. 5c ea.; $3.00 per 100.

—FISTULOSA ALBA.—A white-flowered variety. 5c ea.; $3.00 per 100.

Phalaris.—ARUNDINACEA VAR.—(Variegated Ribbon Grass.) An excellent grass for bordering large beds of Cannas or other tall growing plants. Bright variegations of white and green, retained throughout the season and does not flower. We can highly recommend it as a border plant. 5c ea.; $3.00 per 100.

Phlox.—None of our perennials will give such a wealth of flowers and variety of color as the Phloxes, either in groups or hardy border. They are always in bloom, adapting themselves to any color. We consider the following the best of their color:

—COQUELICOT.—Fine pure scarlet, with deep carmine eye.

—ECLAIREUR.—Purplish crimson, with white halo.

—ETNA.—Scarlet, with dark crimson eye.

—PANTHEON.—Fine deep salmon rose.

—PEACH BLOW.—Delicate pink, with white markings.

—THE PEARL.—A good free white. Large trusses.

Price of the above, 10c ea.; $6.00 per 100.

We have all the best Helianthus.

Physostegia.—VIRGINICA ALBA.—One of the most beautiful of the midsummer flowering perennials, forming large bushes 3 to 4 ft. high. Long spikes of pure white, tubular flowers. 5c ea.; $4.00 per 100.

Pyrethrum.—HYBRIDUM.—No class of plants will give better satisfaction both as to variety of color and freedom of bloom. The colors range from pure white to deep purple. In mixture, 10c ea.; $6.00 per 100.

Rudbeckia.—GOLDEN GLOW.—A very showy, hardy perennial, growing 6 to 7 ft. high and producing an abundance of bright yellow flowers, which resemble those of the Dahlia in size and general appearance. 5c ea.; $3.00 per 100.

—NEWMANII.—Dark, orange-yellow flowers, with deep purple cone, making it invaluable for cutting. 10c ea.; $4.00 per 100.

—PURPUREA.—One of the most interesting plants among hardy perennials. It is of easy culture, forming large, bushy plants, which produce a constant succession of large, reddish-purple flowers about 4 in. across. Large, brown, cone-shaped center, thickly set with golden tips. 10c ea.; $6.00 per 100.

Salvia.—AZURIA GRANDIFLORA.—A Rocky Mountain specie, 2 to 3 ft. high, producing during August and September pretty sky-blue flowers in the greatest profusion. 10c ea.; $8.00 per 100.

—PRATENSIS.—A common European plant, but seldom seen in cultivation. Flowers in long spikes; color, rich blue. Flowers all summer. A very pretty and attractive plant. 10c ea.; $6.00 per 100.

Sedum.—SPECTABILIS.—A very pretty, erect growing specie, attaining a height of 18 in., with broad, oval, light green foliage. Immense showy heads of handsome rose-colored flowers. Indispensable as a late blooming plant. 10c ea.; $8.00 per 100.

Shasta Daisy.—(CHRYSANTHEMUM LEUCANTHEMUM HYBRIDUM.) Enormous, snowy-white flowers, 4 in. in diameter, and composed of three or more rows of petals. It is perfectly hardy, blooming more abundantly and better flowers each season. Exceedingly strong growth. Unexcelled as a cut flower. No garden should be without it. 15c ea.; $10.00 per 100.

Tritoma.—PFITZERII.—An improvement on Uvaria Grandiflora. The flower spikes are freely produced and often 4 ft. high, with heads of bloom 12 in. long. Rich orange-scarlet, shading to salmon rose on edge. 15c ea.; $10.00 per 100.

Valeriana.—OFFICINALIS.—(Garden Heliotrope.) An old-fashioned garden plant, with large dense clusters of purplish-white flowers on stems 2 to 3 ft. long. The flowers have a strong heliotrope fragrance. Early summer. 5c ea.; $4.00 per 100.

MISCELLANEOUS.

Adiantum.—CAPILLUS VENERIS.—One of the best for fern dishes and other decorative work, being of easy culture and hardy constitution. It will thrive under most any treatment and temperature. 5c ea.; $3.00 per 100.

—CAPILLUS VENERIS IMBRICATA.—More dwarf than the above and has larger individual leaflets. Has the appearance of a dwarf Farleyense. 10c ea.; $5.00 per 100.

Asparagus.—PLUMOSUS NANUS.—(Lace Fern.) A very graceful climber, with fine lace-like foliage. Very useful for home decoration as well as for florists' use. Ready May 1st. 5c ea.; $4.00 per 100.

—SPRENGERII.—(Emerald Feather.) A vigorous growing variety, making numerous long, drooping branches. Very useful for hanging baskets. 5c ea.; $3.00 per 100.

—TENUISSIMUS.—Fine, feathery foliage, similar to Plumosus. Useful as a window plant being of easy culture and quite hardy. 5c ea.; $4.00 per 100.

Begonia.—GLORIE DE LORRAINE.—A very free flowering variety, with compact, dwarf growth. The plants are completely covered with clear pink flowers to such an extent that the foliage is usually hidden. It is undoubtedly one of the most useful Christmas plants now in existence. Strong, young plants, ready June 1st, 20c ea.; $15.00 per 100.

—LIGHT PINK LORRAINE.—A beautiful light pink sport from the above variety, but a more vigorous grower. A counterpart except in color. 20c ea.; $15.00 per 100.

—INCARNATA.—This is one of the best varieties among Begonias, being of the easiest culture, and produces its light pink flowers in the greatest profusion. It is a valuable Christmas plant, as it is at its best the latter part of December. 5c ea.; $4.00 per 100.

Get some of Burbank's Floral Wonder,
"SHASTA DAISY."

—Manicata Aurea.—Heavy, waxy leaves, blotched and marbled rich golden cream. Clear pink etchings. Produces light pink flowers on long stems. The finest decorative plant imaginable. 10c ea.; $8.00 per 100.

—Rex.—One of the most beautiful foliage plants for house and conservatory. Our collection includes the best standard varieties. 10c ea.; $5.00 per 100.

Carax.—Japonica Var.—A variegated grass, very desirable for borders, rockeries and basket work. It also makes a pretty plant for the table or conservatory. It is quite hardy and not affected by drought; 10 in. high. 5c ea.; $3.00 per 100.

Coleus.—Thyrsoideus.—(Flowering Coleus. New.) Distinct from other Coleus, from the fact that it is a winter-flowering plant, flowering from Christmas until late in April. The plant is of sturdy growth and plain green foliage; height, 2 to 2½ ft. Dense cylindrical spikes, 1 in. in diameter and from 6 to 12 in. long, bearing rich blue flowers. Very beautiful and attractive. 5c ea.; $4.00 per 100.

Cyperus.—Alternifolious.—(Umbrella Plant.) 5c ea.; $3.00 per 100.

Ferns.—Nephrolepis Bostoniensis.—One of the best and most popular ferns in existence. Long, arching fronds, 2 to 3 ft. in length. Of very easy culture. 5c ea.; $3.00 per 100.

—Cordata Compacta.—A very fine fern for house culture, being a free, healthy grower. Growth, very compact, dwarf, and of a beautiful deep green. 5c ea.; $3.00 per 100.

Feverfew.—(Matricaria.) An indispensable plant to the florist, being very useful for cutting and floral work. It also blooms well in the garden. 5c ea.; $2.50 per 100.

Gladiolus.—Finest mixed, all colors. Good, large bulbs. 25c per doz.; $1.50 per 100.

Ipomea.—(Moonflower.) A beautiful summer climber, 15 to 20 ft. high; makes excellent shade for verandas, also used for covering lattice work. Large, trumpet-shaped, snow-white flowers. 5c ea.; $3.00 per 100.

Isolepis.—Gracilis.—A grass-like plant, very useful for ferneries and hanging baskets. Long, reed-like, drooping blades; center erect. 5c ea.; $3.00 per 100.

Lemon Verbena.—The leaves have a delightful lemon fragrance. Fine for bouquet work. 5c ea.; $3.00 per 100.

Poinsettia.—Pulcherrima.—Very desirable for Christmas decorations, as it produces its large, bright scarlet bracts just at that season. Young plants ready the last of June. 10c ea.; $6.00 per 100.

Salvia Splendens.—Freudenfeuer.—Free, branching habit; 2½ ft. high. Produces an abundance of rich crimson flowers in large, perfect trusses. 5c ea.; $3.00 per 100.

—Gigantea.—This is a grand variety. As its name implies, it is much stronger than the type, attaining 3½ ft. in height, and producing brilliant trusses of extraordinary size. 5c ea.; $3.00 per 100.

—Glory of Stuttgart.—Strong, branching habit; 2 ft. high. Produces immense trusses of bright scarlet flowers in profusion throughout the season. 5c ea.; $3.00 per 100.

—Golden Leaf.—A grand variety, either as a border, or in groups. Bright yellow foliage similar to that of Golden Bedder Coleus. Bushy plants, topped with perfect clusters of brilliant scarlet blooms. The contrast is striking and beautiful. 5c ea.; $3.00 per 100.

—Mrs. Stevens.—Robust, dwarf growth; well branched. Deep green foliage and stems. Deep purple flower of large size. This variety when planted with Golden Leaf and the other varieties, makes one of the prettiest beds imaginable. 5c ea.; $3.00 per 100.

—Patens.—A beautiful half-hardy variety. The flowers are very large and of a bright gentian blue. The most popular blue-flowered salvia and an ornament to every garden. 10c ea.; $6.00 per 100.

—Triumph.—(New.) A very dwarf, free-flowering variety, commencing to flower soon after planted and continues a mass of bloom until frost. Color, rich scarlet, in long, compact trusses. Best of recent introductions. 10c ea.; $5.00 per 100.

Smilax.—Strong plants from 2¼ in. pots, 5c ea.; $2.50 per 100.

Sweet Alyssum.—Double, far superior to the single variety. 5c ea.; $2.50 per 100.

Vinca.—Major Var.—Half hardy trailer. Glossy green leaves, broadly margined and blotched creamy white. One of the very best trailing plants for vases and other filling, where vines may be used. 5c ea.; $3.00 per 100.

NOTICE.

Those desiring the benefit of our experience in making a collection, can rely on our judgment entirely, and advise us as to color, type, time of flowering, etc.

We are in receipt of many communications complimenting the quality of stock, mode of packing, and liberal count, from numerous patrons of last season.

Should you have friends who require plants, we will gladly forward them our catalogue on receipt of their address.

DOUBLE ARCH CARNATION SUPPORT.

This support is giving satisfaction wherever used. After trying very near every other method in use, we have come to the conclusion that this support is the best and cheapest.

ITS CHIEF ADVANTAGES ARE:

1. Its cheapness. 2. The ease with which it can be set, or taken down and stored. 3. Being held rigid by overhead wires, the support is not easily displaced. 4. The plants are never crowded, but kept in a free, natural position. 5. The flowers can be cut on any length stem without disarranging the support. 6. The bed can be watered without wetting any part of the plants. 7. A free circulation of air can always be maintained, thereby checking various diseases. 8. As the arches are made from the very best galvanized wire, they are practically non-destructible.

As seen in illustration, it requires 2 stakes or arches to support each plant. The stakes as quoted are 25 inches in length and 3 in. wide at the top. These are set at right angles over the plant, forming a structure very similar to an oil or wind-mill derrick, as shown in illustration. By spreading or drawing in, the base of the stake can be adjusted to accommodate any plant, either large or small. To keep the support in position, run a light galvanized wire (No. 18 or 20 preferred) lengthwise of the bench, touching the tops of the supports and tie at the crossing of the three wires with raffia or other tying material. We use raffia for enclosing the plants, wrapping it once around each wire to prevent it slipping down. You can tie as often as the size and strength of the plants require. Every few days the growing tips may be tucked inside the raffia enclosure. As the plants are in a free, upright position, the flowers can be easily cut with full length stems. The cost of setting the supports is reduced to a minimum, and when not in use, they take up no more room than a coil of wire.

The following quotations are per **100 arches,** and it requires **two** of these to support **each plant:** No. 11 Wire, bent ready for use, $1.15 per 100. No. 9 Wire, bent ready for use, $1.30 per 100. F. O. B. Adrian. In making order, state plainly whether you are referring to **arches** or the **complete support,** as it requires **two** of the former to make **one** of the latter.

The above quotations are subject to change without notice, as price of wire fluctuates continually.

After careful tests we find that the 25 inch stake is the best suited for most varieties of Carnations. If shorter stakes than those quoted are desired, subtract 10 cents for every 3 inch deduction in length, and for longer stakes add 10 cents for every additional 3 inches.

Rose, Chrysanthemum, and other plant stakes, cut to any length, will be quoted on application.

All *The* Best

Chrysanthemums
Carnations
Cannas

Nephrolepis Piersoni.

Pelargoniums
Geraniums
Etc.

Correspondence Solicited.

FINCH, PRINTER, ADRIAN, MICH.

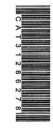